Felix Family Villages

providing a mother and a father
to abandoned children
in the World

Roland Nelsson

© Roland Nelsson
Published by
Felix Family Villages International
P.O. Box 26, SE-57821 ANEBY, Sweden
Produced in cooperation with
International Trading & Consultancy Ltd
and Borneling Publishing House.
Graphic processing, typesetting & cover:
SWH Layout, Aneby, Sweden
3rd revised edition translated into English by Jonathan Newton
1st edition was published in 2004 entitled The vision has landed!
Printed by InterPress, Budapest, Hungary, 2014

ISBN 978 91 7317 199-1

Felix Family Villages

providing a mother and a father
to abandoned children
in the World

Roland Nelsson

Translated by
Jonathan Newton

Foreword by Roland Nelsson

During my many years as Director of Erikshjälpen, I received many applications from various parts of our world. Every now and then, Linda and Lars Hörnberg wrote requests for dialysis machines and other healthcare equipment for Romania. Often, we could respond positively to their letters. In 1988, the great earthquake in Armenia took place. Immediately, Lars Hörnberg contacted us with a request concerning our prospects to support those affected. Yes, of course!

The Soviet Embassy consul in Stockholm, Alexander Kudinov, open all the doors for us, and Lars and I travel there between Christmas and the New Year and handed over about SEK 300,000 as a first effort. After that, a steady stream of supplies flowed from Holsbybrunn to those affected by the earthquake in Leninakan, Artyk and Goukassian. Amongst other things, we've built up an entire village, a preschool, and donated medical equipment to the hospitals. At about this time, the EPRO – the Pentecostal Movements' European Aid Organization – was formed, founded by Pastor John Wildrianne and backed by Pastor Brian Edwards, both prominent figures in the two English Pentecostal movements Assemblies of God and Elim Church. All the different Pentecostal movements in Europe joined the EPRO, and contributed, amongst other things, to the rebuilding of the Goukassian village in Armenia.

Many things happened in connection with that project. Armenia became the largest challenge for us ever since I joined Erikshjälpen. It was about this time the doctor told me that I had a malign cancer tumor in my chest. God touched me, and after surgery and intercession, this deadly disease was removed from me. This is now 25 years ago!

Armenia thus became a milepost for me. I suppose you could say that Lars Hörnberg indirectly contributed to that experience. After all, he put us on track, so to say, and opened up the Soviet Union to Swedish aid efforts. Then came the events in Romania and the fall of Ceausescu. The execution of the Ceausescus was shown on TV. Soon, the situation for the Romanian children was revealed. On Christmas Eve itself in 1989, I had summoned the board of Erikshjälpen for a conference call, and we decided to try to do something for the children of Romania, perhaps in the same manner as we had done in Armenia.

Since then, I have followed the events and the development of Caminul Felix. It is now 25 years since the adventure started. Many times, I have wished that I could write down what happened in Romania for a Swedish audience. A few years ago, I heard Lars Hörnberg at a service on Wednesday night in the Pentecostal church in Landsbro exclaim emotionally: "I have seen more miracles than anyone else has done!" Yes, perhaps more wanted to read and see what Lars had seen!

Doreen and John Wildrianne

The miracles that Lars has seen and which I can confirm, are those that I have now tried to write down. I have gained much help from a good friend in England, Doreen Wildrianne, who, a few years ago, published her book "The Heart and the Vision – The Story of Caminul Felix, new hope for abandoned children". Her book is sold in England and the U.S.

Doreen is the wife of Pastor John Wildrianne, the founder of the EPRO (European Pentecostal Relief Organisation) which was formed a few years before the disastrous earthquake in Armenia. Erikshjälpen became one of the supporting aid organizations of the EPRO. I count Doreen and John Wildrianne among my personal friends.

In 2009, John died suddenly. He had just said farewell to his Bible College students at the International Bible Training Institute when the Lord called my dear brother home to glory.

Since the start of the International Bible Training Institute in Sussex, England, Doreen Wildrianne has been the leading personality at the school. It is here several of those carrying the responsibilities within Caminul Felix have received their further education. These include Linda Hörnberg and Lisa Egerbo whom the reader will meet in the book.

The present book is partly based on the research that Doreen so meritoriously has done, and I have revised and translated a few chapters from English for a Swedish audience.
Berndt Sanfridson, who, together with his wife, Elise, heads the Foundation Caminul Felix Sweden, has been a driving force for the book to be written.

The book aims at being a presentation of individuals who have stepped forward to build up a devastated country. They believe that God has called them to this. Their efforts will surely be judged by history as absolutely crucial for how Romania changed its policy towards its rising generation and thus got on to its feet as an entire nation, even though there is still much work that remains to be done.

Lars Hörnberg says that God asked a carpenter to become the

adoptive father of his son, and Joseph gave the world an image of how a true father-son relation could be. God gave the world's most important job to the simplest of people, to Mary and Joseph, who had no previous experience of being parents. And, of course, no other new parents have any experience of that either. The world's most important task is to be a parent and nobody has that experience from the beginning.

Radiana Tiplea – one of the new mothers – stands in her living room, looking out through the window and thinking out loud: "I often stand here seeing the children playing here outside together with the other children at Caminul Felix, and I wonder: 'What would have become of them if they hadn't been saved out of their humiliation and come to us? Perhaps they wouldn´t been alive today.' I have never regretted my decision to become a mother to my children!"

One of the fathers – Mircea Toca – exclaims: "What I've learned from Linda and Lars Hörnberg and the other leaders here are things that I would never have learned at any university! Caminul Felix is Life's Own University!" Join us on the exciting journey to Caminul Felix – Life's Own University!

* * *

The chapter division is not always in a chronological order. Therefore, I will list the events from 1989 here below:

1989 Elena and Nicolae Ceausescu were executed
1990 Linda and Lars Hörnberg deepen their collaboration with Erikshjälpen
1991 Caminul Felix 1 under construction.
1992 Caminul Felix 1 inaugurated
1994 Casa Minunata opened
1995 Construction of the farm is begun

1996	Action Felix is formed
1999	Theranova is build
1999	An International Board is formed with Bob Pagett as Chairman
2000	Caminul Felix 2 under construction
2001	Caminul Felix 2 inaugurated
2002	The Foundation Caminul Felix Sweden formed
2003	The Teenage House under construction
2006	The Teenage House inaugurated
2006	Decision about starting ministry in Thailand
2009	Felix Family Village in Surat Thani, Thailand, is inaugurated

Foreword by Lars Hörnberg

I see the facts that are not detected yet for the public of our world, that the 165 million abandoned children in the world are the most outcast of all groups and categories of people today.

They were born not wanted and they have no legacy to expect. They are totally poor and lost. They are kicked around physically, marginalized socially, expected to not to breath and ask for anything emotionally. They are basically without chance to an education, although some make - it praise the Lord. They do not get access to the environment that is given by a loving family and provides the surrounding making an individual bloom and becoming the person God intended, which is there in the heart and mind of the little ones. Not wanted, predetermined for destitution, for ever mentally and emotionally marked and rejected.

I believe that speaks about the incredible responsibility the parent generation has now.

The hope is in awareness of responsibility by a mature society, commitment to sponsor these little one's rights to family and a full life by the parent generation.

There is one hope for all, and that is the awareness of our role and calling to the next generation, a mandatory involvement and enlisting to rescue them, and a loving heart that is wide open to the everybody's calling to purpose and reasons for living. There is a massive need for heart and knowledge.

The author's thanks and tribute to the Sponsors

You heard about Jennie, 4 years old, who gave her pacifier to Romania's crying children!

But do you know what happened next?
I know!
I have seen Caminul Felix and I am almost dumbstruck!
This is how it was and this is how it turned out:

- Jennie from Eksjö donated her pacifier and thus realized the idea of the Family Village Caminul Felix in Romania!
- Erikshjälpen spread the word about the matter and invested heavily during the construction phase!
- Team Boro AB built homes!
- Björhags Måleri AB from Värnamo colored the houses!
- Other companies donated white goods, locks and paint for huge sums of money!
- From Sweden and the U.S., hundreds of volunteers came and built family homes!
- At an old cemetery in Oradea, the Teenage House took form!
- A retired farmer from the U.S. developed land into the best farm in Transylvania with billowing cornfields!
- A dairy with cheese production of its own!
- The Lions Club in Sweden financed Casa Minunata (The House of Miracles) and gave the disabled a new perspective of their future!
- An individual donated funds to the prosthetic limbs workshop Theranova (New Therapy) and many severely

disabled young people rose from the floor or their wheelchairs!
- Martin Luther King dreamed about the Promised Land. Linda and Lars Hörnberg did the same about Romania!
- Now, there are dreams for an Academy for education of parent couples from all over the world! Surely that dream will come true!
- Many sponsors each month donate their important money and ostracized children have a home, school education and healthcare!

I want to pay tribute to those of you who are donors and sponsors and I am convinced about your continued support! You form the basis for a project that is unique from a sponsoring point of view! Not only Romania and Thailand pay tribute to you, other countries cast jealous glances at what you are doing for children in vulnerable situations!

Content

Forewords by Roland Nelsson and Lars Hörnberg
The author´s thanks and tributes to sponsors

Chapter

1

The Emperor and the Dictator

Had Nicolae Ceausescu listened to the old wise Emperor Haile Selassie of Ethiopia, perhaps Romania would have had a different development than the one we got to know. The Emperor Haile Selassie of Ethiopia invited Nicolae Ceausescu with his wife Elena to his beautiful country. In the itinerary that the Emperor presented to the Ceausescu couple, a visit to the Swedish Pentecostal Mission in Awassa was also included.

* * *

For decades, Sweden had had deep and friendly relation with Ethiopia. Sweden had warm sentiments towards the country and the commitment to Ethiopia was well-known both to the Swedish and Ethiopian public. It felt so right to both parties to hold on to and also to deepen that collaboration. Who hadn't heard about the Red Cross's White Buses from Sweden, which, at the end of the Abyssinian war in the mid-1930s, had sought to ease the suffering for refugees and those injured in the war? Who hadn't heard about the Ethiopian air force, which, some decades later, had been developed by Swedish instructors? Telecommunications in the country had been built by the Swedes. In the 60s, SIDA (The Swedish International Development Cooperation Agency) assisted in modernizing the expansion of the Ethiopian education system. A Finland-Swede, Niskanen, was behind the Ethiopian Marathon athletes' success in the Olympics. That is, not to mention von Rosen's food bombings during the famine disaster in 1984.

* * *

The two heads of state, Nicolae Ceausescu and Haile Selassie, were well respected in their respective countries, but also internationally. From President Richard Nixon in the USA, it was heard that Ceausescu would give the Soviet Iron Curtain builders a match. Romania would become the front of Eastern Europe with good connections among the democratic states in the West. Did the Emperor, with his invitation to Ceausescu, play a part in the European development? It is possible. The Emperor had long experience and knew both what Europe could and wanted to do with the intention to raise the living standards for the countries in the southern hemisphere. When Benito Mussolini had tried to annex Ethiopia so as to provide Italy with its own granary, Haile Selassie travelled to the meeting of the League of Nations in Berlin. There, he made a dramatic appeal to the European conscience to stop Italy's aggression against his country. In the 60s, the Emperor noted the positive events in Europe. He invited Yugoslavia's President Tito and even his former archenemy Italy, whose experts were welcome to continue to develop Ethiopia.

In Romania, Nicolae Ceausescu had just been elected President when the invitation came from Haile Selassie to visit Ethiopia. "When we reach Awassa, I would like to show you what Swedish foreign aid can accomplish," said Haile Selassie to his guest

Nicolae Ceausescu just before the car trip from the capital Addis Ababa was begun in a couple of fine, black limousines. They put the 270 kilometers to Awassa behind them in about three hours on the only paved road in the country. Skånska Cement – as Skanska was then named – had constructed the road at the end of the 50s. Upon arrival in Awassa, they were met by the Swedish missionaries at the Black River which constituted the northern city limits.

The Swedish vocational school with its teachers and some 50 boys had, ahead of the state visit, been working hard with giving their Emperor and his European guests a dignified reception. An arch of arranged eucalyptus had been set up over the bridge whose parapets were also decorated with beautiful, freshly picked wild flowers that the surrounding grounds were strewn with.

From the first limousine, the Emperor stepped out and greeted students and teachers. From the second limousine, Ceausescu and his wife Elena emerged. It actually looked as if the Emperor felt proud of the Swedish missionary corps standing there dressed up and at attention when he introduced it to Ceausescu.

It became quite a welcoming ceremony.

Later in the afternoon, they met again, this time at the vocational school. The school's founder Karl Ramstrand presented the four vocational educations: construction technology, metal mechanics, a carpentry school and a motor car garage.

The missionaries had taken the opportunity to place Bibles in strategic places on the school's premises.

"What are these books lying about here and there?" asked Haile Selassie. He certainly knew what the answer would be, when one of the missionaries. Gudrun Nelsson, answered:

"These are Bibles, honorable Emperor. Every morning, the

entire school assembles for devotion, and the Bible is then our textbook."

"Good," said the Emperor. It is important that my young people also get to know what the Word of God teaches. It is incredibly important with vocational training. But the development of my country will benefit from it being built on a Christian foundation," the Emperor continued.

The young missionaries experienced the Emperor's words as a powerful recognition and a confirmation to the call to build the country on a Christian ideology.

Ceausescu had no questions to ask. He almost looked embarrassed about the Emperor's commendatory words to the missionaries.

Had Ceausescu listened to the old wise Emperor Haile, perhaps Romania would have had a different development than the one we got to know.

The Emperor only had a few more years to reign before a bloody, Communist revolution devastated the country.

* * *

There is one group of people on Earth that has a very special mission. They are the most remarkable people on the planet. They are not a majority and they are rarely on state agencies in authority. They are not well-paid, on the contrary. Many of them are completely ordinary and hard-working professional people, some with impressive education. Common to them all is that they are Readers[1], readers of the Bible book. 'Missionaries' is another and more common concept for this group of people.

"Make all nations into My disciples…"

---

1   The Swedish word for "Reader" has historically also had the additional meaning of referring to Swedish Pietism Christians, for being fervent Bible readers. *–Translator's note*

What a mission!

Is it even possible?

These people have a look on their eyes that is hard to explain, they are sort of looking into the future. They are a class to themselves. I remember from my own childhood when the missionaries visited my church or stayed overnight at my simple parental home. They spoke about countries and parts of the world that were far away, on the other side of the globe. They felt responsible for capitals with millions of inhabitants. They said that their mission was to save the heathens. Much later, I understood what they actually meant by that. Their mission was to establish peace between different tribes and peoples. Their mission was to lift entire nations to a better social consciousness. Their mission was to mediate between warring parties. Their mission was to provide education. Their mission was to heal the sick. That awareness had been born within them while reading the book that is the most spread one globally, the Bible. In addition, they had heard an inner prompting to give their lives in this mission. They said that God had called them.

These people are the most remarkable ones in the world. They had not been nominated to any political party's ballot list. They had no thoughts of seizing earthly power by coups d'état.

* * *

When Ceausescu just before Christmas in 1989 appeared on the tribune in Bucharest to speak to the people, he had the surprise of his life. The people booed him. A few days later, he was no longer in the land of the living. Neither was his wife still alive. Both were atrociously executed in front of the eyes of the world. We saw it on TV.

President Nicolae Ceausescu and his Elena should have listened to a wise old Emperor in Africa!

Chapter

2

Two Missionary Candidates

It was great news that the Hutchens family had been blessed with yet another baby girl. Perhaps the event was not covered by the nation with hopes for the transformation of society, but the new baby would nevertheless later change many hundreds of people's lives.

From her mother's arms, the little girl could see a wonderful view outside her bedroom window. The Californian landscape bore witness to God's creating care as far as the eye could see, but little did she suspect that there was a world farther away. Little could she have already understood that God would lead her from country to country and finally to an unknown destination.

Her parents called her Linda.

She was born on November 1, 1949, as the third child of the family. Her brother and sister were quite a few years older. The home was in Reedley, California in the United States.

Linda's father, Milton Hutchens, worked as a foreman at a large farm north of Visalia, and later as a planner at a lumber industry in Dinuba. Milton was a strongman and worked hard to provide for his family. Later, he opened a furniture store together with his wife, and they ran it together for 15 years. But it was not only for the sake of business they opened their company. There was a higher goal than to make money. Their way of life as Christians was respected by the people in the community. They were quick to help people who were worse off.

Lois Hutchens stayed at home during Linda's childhood and only worked occasionally away from home. A better task is probably hard to find for a mother than for her to give her time to taking care of the home and raising the children.

The parents were active in church with various commissions of trust, board functions, being Sunday school principals and teachers. All three children made decisions for the Lord early on. Their parents had taught them to trust in God.

Milton's and Lois's testimony is that God has provided for them day by day and during all of life's conditions during 65 years of marriage.

Linda was thus given a steady foundation to stand on and her childhood was happy in the Christian environment of her home.

* * *

Far from California's beautiful nature and less than a year before what you know now, another child was born who would play an important role. In a town in Sweden with 30,000 inhabitants, Bollnäs, Lars Hörnberg entered into this world.

* * *

Lars's father, Bo Hörnberg, had eventually become one of the most famous pastors within the Swedish Pentecostal movement. For many years, he was Pastor Lewi Pethrus's collaborator in Stockholm. When he later became Senior Pastor of the large congregation in Jönköping with more than two thousand members, he made himself known as a huge friend of the Christians in Eastern Europe. Bosse – as his friends called him – made many journeys throughout Europe and he also called pastors from behind the Iron Curtain to visit the annual "Preachers' Days" in Jönköping, with thousands of participants from large parts of Sweden.

It was no secret that someone in the invited group of preachers from the Soviet Union was a so-called "informant" for the KGB. We even knew who that person was, but he was always met with the same warmth and love as the rest of the group. But the "informant's" boldness never reached far enough for him to take the pulpit in Jönköping!

When invited pastors arrived from the Soviet Union, they had an imperative duty to hold a speech for peace at some point in Sweden. This was a requirement from the Soviet authorities for them to allow the pastors their travel visas. Bosse believed that such a speech would not be appreciated in a pastors' conference. The visiting pastors agreed. After all, they were there to share about another dimension of fellowship and not to hold a political speech. That could be perceived as a justification of the "Evil Empire," as Ronald Reagan called the Soviet Union at that time.

The speech for peace that still had to be held was instead always held at the dinner table at Bosse's and his wife Ulla's home. At the dinner table, the "informant" was always present as an invited guest. He could then upon arrival in Moscow guarantee to his superiors that the speech for peace had been held and that the pastors had carried out their task with excellence!

* * *

Bosse's wife Ulla stood by her husband throughout the years even though she had her own livelihood as a bank clerk for more than 30 years.

It was on February 22, 1948, that Ulla and Bo Hörnberg had their first boy. His name was Lars.

* * *

These two children, Linda and Lars, grew up ignorant of each other's' existence, one in an infinite landscape environment in the U.S., the other in Sweden's major cities. Different countries and different languages and cultures.

* * *

To Linda, the ordinary school and college lay before her. Her exceptional singing ability, her gift of music and drama had been discovered early on. As early as at age three, she sang her first solos in church.

As a teenager, Linda was active in the Assembly of God in Reedley, California, where Melvin Harrel was a pastor. Melvin and his wife Millie, who have played an important role in Linda's life, gave her good advice, encouragement and exhortations during youth years that could be tough at times, and who finally led her to full dedication to the Lord Jesus Christ.

It was during a trip to Europe together with Melvin and Millie Harrel and a youth team that Linda gave her life completely to service for the Lord. Later, she understood that it was indeed

Eastern Europe that would become her mission field. She decided to train for her missionary task at the International Bible Training Institute in Sussex, England.

Linda returned to California after her education in England together with a Swedish girl who had also studied at the same school. When she returned home, Melvin Harrel asked if the two girls could consider taking up pioneer work in a Native American reservation where he had previously established some connections. Under incredibly primitive circumstances, the two girls managed to build a lasting Evangelical work which they could later hand over to a young couple.

Europe called once again, and under the congregation's protection, Linda returned to Sweden together with Lotta. She chose Sweden because of the country's easy access to Eastern Europe. First, she had to learn Swedish, and she did that while working in different professions so as to raise the support that would be necessary for her work as a missionary.

With endurance and conviction, Linda built confidence as a singer and evangelist in churches and schools, made TV shows and recorded LPs together with different teams of musicians.

Eventually, she started travelling to the Soviet Union and other Communist countries behind the iron Curtain, not always in safe conditions and sometimes under outright dangerous circumstances.

There would be many years of successful activity for Linda Hutchens.

* * *

Lars was a steady and conscientious boy, diligent in his studies

11

and in his thirst for knowledge.

To an outside observer, it is interesting to understand how Lars already as a schoolboy would help weaker and less equipped students. He had an innate sense of empathy and commitment to his peers. Without a doubt, this sense grew out of the strong Christian family that he came from. He learned to practice Jesus's teachings.

His father said:
"As a young man, Lars was eager to evangelize and win people for God. Often, he would wake up already at five o'clock in the morning, and spend some time in prayer. My kid led a rich prayer life."

After finishing school, he studied at the Bible College in Stockholm. Then, theological studies waited at Southern California College, Costa Mesa, California in the United States.

Lars was only 20 years old when he started his career as a pastor. For seven years, he was a Bible teacher in his own congregation in Malmö. For a while, he also taught at Mariannelund, one of the Pentecostal movement's four folk high schools. For many years, he served as a pastor in different congregations in Sweden.

All of this of course seems to have been dead straight, but that is not what life is like. Soldiers are trained in combat and endurance before being sent on the battlefield. Such tests also took place in Lars's life. What he had received from home of trust in God and during his early years of prayer and evangelization, refined the call to win people for God. Lars learned that circumstances can place a servant of God, too, in dead ends.

The thought of countries and peoples outside of his own

country was slowly taking shape.

In a recent interview, Lars said:

"Already before meeting Linda, I went on extensive preaching trips in eastern Europe. I was called to conferences in the Soviet Union, Hungary and Poland and later also to South America and Africa. But it was Eastern Europe that gripped my heart and I made an infinite number of contacts with church leaders in many eastern European countries."

For a few years, Lars thus made a large number of contacts with Christian leaders and humanitarian organizations in Sweden and throughout the world. When you consider Lars's career, you cannot then pass over the large disaster that hit Armenia in 1988. The largest earthquake in modern times had devastated a number of large cities, and many thousands of people were severely affected. Lars contacted the Soviet ambassador in Stockholm and offered his services. The ambassador accepted the offer and opened up the country for Swedish foreign aid efforts. The effort that was made was expanded considerably when the EPRO – the European Pentecostal movement's foreign aid organization – stepped in with its large support.

Lars and Linda Hörnberg

Lars contacted organizations, congregations, and municipalities, and tons of supplies were driven to the earthquake area. As a result of Lars's vision, today, there are again functioning hospitals, schools, and churches. The international humanitarian effort that was born because of the Armenian disaster had the good thing about it that the relations with countries and congregation leaders in Europe were deepened. Romania came into focus. Romania, however, was nothing new to Lars and Linda. Both of them had previous warm ties to the country, mainly with congregations and their pastors, but also with hospitals in the county of Bihor.

Lars says:
"We handed over lots of fine medical equipment which opened new doors into the Romanian society. That was quite an unusual way in which to reach Romanian society. We didn't come as representatives of some churches, but as friends for those in need, which was unusual for those who used to travel to Romania."

* * *

Now, the differences had been united. Only God could bring two people together – so different when it came to background and culture. Lars and Linda Hörnberg embarked together on a common journey to convey hope where there is only darkness and desperation.

Chapter
3

"There will always be a Falköping"

The expression in the headline comes from Lars Hörnberg. The Pentecostal congregation in Falköping plays a completely crucial role in Linda's and Lars Hörnberg's lives. There are no doubts whatsoever about that. It is Falköping that has left its mark on the missionary deeds that Linda and Lars are doing in Romania. It is also there they have returned to from their journeys in Eastern Europe. But there are things that mean even more to Linda and Lars. It is in the Pentecostal Church in Falköping that they have been able to fetch mental and spiritual strength when the world around them has been unfair and harsh. Life is not always easy. Nobody escapes hard knocks, especially not those who have an important task to perform. "But then, there will always be a Falköping," as Lars Hörnberg said. In the previous chapter, there were some indications that Lars's "career" as a pastor had not always been straightforward at circumstances sometimes can place a servant of God into a dead end. Let me go back some 35 years and give a condensed explanation about what had happened to Lars a few years before he met Linda:

It was at the Pentecostal movement's "Preachers' Week" in Stockholm, which takes place in December every year. Lars was always one of the participants. I often used to see him walk through the packed church to take his place at the very front, often accompanied by his father, Bo Hörnberg. I also saw him during that "week" which became his last for many years. That was the year when the pastors decided to appoint a "care group". There was a perceived need to care for tired and worn out pastors who, in one way or another, needed to change churches. Then, the care group could help out. But Lars Hörnberg would not be included in that care. He had gone through a divorce, and for a pastor who could not keep his marriage together, the care group's resources were not enough at this time within the Pentecostal movement. Lars felt excluded from the fellowship of pastors. That was at the beginning of the 1980s.

Lars was struggling. He worked as a teacher at the Mariannelund folk high school. He sold art. The time as a pastor was over. No colleague contacted him and no congregation wanted to hear him preach. But it was then that some good friends of Linda's made sure that Lars got a job as a janitor in Linköping. So Lars swept staircases in large apartment buildings for a year or so.

After a year with the broom in the staircase, Lars and Linda were invited to the Falköping Pentecostal church. That became the "E.R.," as Lars puts it. Lars had thus met Linda, who had been working together with the congregation in Falköping for many years. At some times, Linda had been in Romania and other eastern European countries. When the huge earthquake shook Romania in 1977, Linda was one of the first ones to drive into the country with supplies to those affected.

Lars was called to the Pentecostal church in Falköping as a colleague of Pastor Christer Zethsson. The door was opened again for Lars to preach. The congregation's elders consisted of tender counselors and board members who welcomed Lars with open arms. Confidence had returned. Apart from serving in the congregation, Lars was also called to travel in the East. Linda introduced Lars to her friends in Romania, and soon, the new country took up an increasing amount of their time. Lars and Linda got married in 1985.

"It was exclusively Linda's work in Romania that made me come here," Lars says when I met him in Oradea. "To me, Linda's connections in Romania became the Spirit's guidance into a fantastic mission."

Chapter

4

Ceausescu is dead – save the children!

At last it has been revealed! The devilish, heartbreaking secret about the miserable conditions for Romania's tens of thousands of abandoned children is being displayed to a surprised world. Other disgraces are also out in the open, but it is the children's situation that upsets the world.

It was in December, 1989, that the truth about Communist Romania became front-page news in the media all over the world. Nicolae Ceausescu, supported and encouraged by his similarly ruthless wife, Elena, had now ruled the country with exceptionally corrupt nepotism for 25 years. The country was governed with ever-increasing repression and with consistent depletion of the nation.

The Ceausescu couple was ousted in a revolutionary coup in December, 1989, and both were executed after a summary trial. Then, one revelation after another followed of what had happened in Romania during their time. Nobody had had a clue about what had been going on in the national darkness, not even among the majority of the Romanian people.

Ceausescu is dead! The world has heard the truth! Now the children must be saved!

Lars Hörnberg tells the story:
"Only a few weeks after the revolution, we traveled to Romania. We contacted the congregations that we knew of since before. We understood that the ordinary citizens did not know what had been going on in the country. Well, in one place or another, people had probably heard but kept quiet, the secret was dirty and shameful. There was no compassion – the children were forgotten. They had been hidden away behind closed doors. They were left in evil hands and we soon understood that the church leaders did not know of these multitudes of abandoned children either.

We came from the free world and found that Romania was a closed society and therefore, our entire perspective became so completely different. Linda and I perceived our situation as unique in such a way that our previous relations and contacts now became even more important and we could now develop these much more clearly. We saw children in the streets who had escaped from the state orphanages and we understood that something had to be done. At the moment we realized that, the insight became an issue that became dear to our hearts. Others said: 'We are thinking of you but we do not want to get involved.'

We visited hospitals and institutions and what we saw was more than you could endure. Somebody had to do something! The disastrous situation became our responsibility. We only had our own small apartment, but it was there everything started and the first abandoned child had its first home. Before too long, we had seven of these abandoned and destitute children at home.

It started so simply. We simply could not help doing it. Our commitment grew and eventually became an incredible blessing when we saw the change in these children's lives and in their families.

That is how Caminul Felix evolved. It started in one little apartment and soon became a children's village with six homes that could give shelter to many of the abandoned children that nobody had previously cared about.

We became the first ones to build a 'Children's Home' in the country; the first effort to meet the enormous needs that existed in the country. It was an incredible challenge to fetch the children from their miserable situation and try to get them into acceptable conditions, especially as the new society in no way was ready to accept or take care of them. The children were bullied and their lives were actually in danger. But we knew what needed to be done!"

Gudrun Nelsson (right) came to be responsible for the sponsoring activities to Caminul Felix. Here she is seen with a young Romani mother.

* * *

A large celebration was held in the streets of Oradea on the Day of Independence. Linda Hörnberg was there and stepped up to the microphone. Her rich and beautiful alto voice flowed out over the multitudes when she, touched by the country's new freedom, sang her heart out in the song "Our Father". The multitudes cheered and joined in with the song, they were free!

Linda also has her story to tell about how things came into place:

"When the doors were opened to Romania in connection with the revolution in 1989, we were there. We had perhaps understood partly what the situation was like in the state institutions which had been closed to the public through all the years. These institutions were the homes of the abandoned and disabled children.

What we saw was more than we had been able to anticipate. We were shocked and upset about what was behind the closed doors. The children were kept like animals in cages, tied to their beds. What we saw was more than we could manage to take in. In one place, we found 80 boys in such a misery that I have described. They stretched out their desperate hands towards us and pleaded 'love us' because in all their misery, it was love they longed for!

Siblings with a common future.

You do not need to think for long about why this cruel regime fell. The

22

regime's attitude towards the young people of the country was so cynical and terrifying and as far from humanity and Evangelical love that you could get. Jesus had showed a completely different attitude when he took the children into his arms, showered them with love and condemned those who harmed the children in any way.

Lars and I immediately felt that we wanted to create a completely new way of caring for the country's children. We went to the churches' leaders who said that they had no money for any measures. But if God was with us in our thoughts, he would make sure that means would come in. At that moment, we did not have any organization behind us, so we decided to go straight to the county governor with our thoughts. He immediately gave us a large piece of land where we would be able to realize our vision!"

* * *

Now, the pieces were coming together – seven children in an apartment and a piece of land in the Sanmartin village outside Oradea. "The Hörnberg Vision," which, when completed, would become a family village, filled with children who had come over from death to life. Now with a mother and a father, siblings, yes, with everything that belongs to a child in a normal world.

The God-given vision was there; the sincerity of their hearts was there and kept the vision alive. Linda's and Lars's conviction would eventually turn the vision into a unit. But how would that happen?

Perhaps you could not expect any support from Romanian congregations or municipalities. It is only God who can give birth to a miracle in somebody's heart, somewhere!

The distance home to Sweden was not very far, the country

that had sent out Lars and Linda as its missionaries to the different places in Eastern Europe and now finally to Romania.

It was at that moment I was contacted by Linda and Lars. God had prepared many miracles in Sweden, and Erikshjälpen became the sluice through which these would flow out to Romania. Read, for example, about Jennie!

Chapter
5

Jennie's pacifier

Nicolae Ceausescu had failed to do it. The Swedish government would try later, but would be incapable of it.

Then came Jennie's pacifier.

The pacifier turned up on my desk one morning. It came in a letter from the post office clerk Kennet Palm in Nässjö together with a little message:

"The pacifier was found in a mailbox which was emptied on my sorting table a few days ago. I have been moved to tears by what I have read on the note, but I have not known what to do with it until now, and that is why I have sent it to you at Erikshjälpen."

Well, what was I supposed to do? I also understood a certain connection when I read the note that was tied to the pacifier. "For the children in Romania from Jennie," it said. But of course you could not send a severely chewed pacifier to Romania, and you

"To the Romanian children from Jennie"   Photo: Birger Lallo

could not sell it for the benefit of Romania's children either. It would not bring in anything, not even at a charity auction.

The pacifier on my desk stayed for a few days and then I was finished with it and was just about to put it in the trash can. "No, you can't do that," I thought. "I'll have to hang it on the wall as a nice memory."

The day after, it was time to write the "Quarterly Letter." "Well, I can write about the pacifier," I thought! And so I did! I thought up this story about Jennie, age 3, who lived in Nässjö. She had heard about the children in Romania one day and so she asked her mother for help. Mommy and Jennie tied a red ribbon around the pacifier and wrote the greeting on a little note that was also tied to the pacifier. When they got to a mailbox, Mommy lifted Jennie up and she put her pacifier in the mailbox.

Well, that was more or less what I wrote, and sent the letter to Erikshjälpen's readers. The money started pouring in.

Then, Jennie's mother got in touch over the phone.
"Hi, it's Jennie's mother!" she said.

I froze. What would "Mommy" say about my stunt? Had I gone too far? Could you write as I had done? After all, I had tried to portray something that was beautiful. But had I done something wrong?

"Hi, Jennie's mother," I said cautiously, and thought a thousand thoughts. Was "Mommy" on the war path? Well, she had sounded friendly when she greeted me.

"Well, I didn't know that much, it was of course only the pacifier that I had. I hope I wasn't too mistaken?" I wondered.

"No, it was a beautiful story!" said Jennie's mother. "I don't have Erikshjälpen's 'Quarterly Letter,'" she continued, "but my colleague has it, and today, she told me about your story about Jennie and said that it had to be your daughter that Roland was writing about. Later, I saw the article, and I just wanted to call and thank you! The fact that Jennie is 4 ½ years and lives in Eksjö doesn't matter, does it?"

* * *

The "Quarterly Letter" quickly raised about three million crowns, and much money continued to pour in. Lars Hörnberg got in touch again. After all, it was Lars who had brought us into the Armenian work so successfully. Now, Lars and his wife Linda were on location in the city of Oradea in western Romania with an idea to build a children's village together with the Baptist congregation there. We decided to accept Hörnberg's challenge. A few people around me – Göran Ivarsson, Bernt Einarsson and P-O Klint – got started, and after a year or so, the children's village Caminul Felix was completed. Companies from Småland, headed by Boro AB and Swedoor, gave us huge discounts during procurement, and other companies were happy to follow. Professionals from southern Sweden, pensioners or holiday makers, traveled to Oradea, built, painted, electrified and fixed.

* * *

Yet another piece of the jigsaw had come into place. Rumors about what was going on in San Martin spread throughout the Oradea district. Seven houses had been constructed, six out of these were family homes and would be filled with 16 children in each. The seventh house became a multi-purpose building with offices for administration and a medical center as well as an assembly hall for joint meetings, among other things.

It was absolutely clear that the houses could quickly be filled with children who were roaming the streets of Oradea, but how were you to find parents who wanted to take care of 16 abandoned children with all the hassle it would bring?

The connections the Hörnberg's had with the local Christian congregations were of vital importance when house parents were to be recruited. Many people volunteered. Several of the "candidate parents" had children of their own but saw it as God's call to "adopt" yet another batch of kids, 16 of them!

The first ones to move in were the seven ones from Hörnberg's apartment, then soon, all six houses became inhabited. Here, you can really talk about coming from darkness to light, from cold to warmth, from hatred to love, from starvation to overflowing tables, from a life in the sewers to life in a cozy home, from loneliness to a family!

So what does the family village look like? At the center, there is a large green playground surrounded by the dormitories, spread out in a giant horseshoe formation. The houses are painted in different bright colors and every house is surrounded by its own little vegetable garden. Even though the houses are of the same type and style, each house has its own individual atmosphere both on the inside and on the outside.

When you enter any home, you feel straight away – this is a home! They are neat and tidy and have a breathe of hominess. A large living room and, for the children, a number of bedrooms with two beds in each room and an assortment of teddy bears and toys.

Outside, the smaller children are playing, and the older ones are busy with various sports. The grounds are filled with happy voices. Indeed, the children are living a normal life. Everything is a great miracle!

Caminul Felix is no longer only a dream, the dream has come true!

All this about Felix started with Jennie giving her pacifier! What Ceausescu had not been able to do, and not the Swedish Prime Minister and the head of SIDA (Swedish International Development Cooperation Agency), in spite of previous promises that you can read about in the next chapter, Jennie did! She put our faithful donors on track and miracles started pouring in to Caminul Felix!

Chapter
6

Rosenbad

Prime Minister Ingvar Carlsson surprised everybody with an invitation to a seminar at Rosenbad[1]. Those invited were the organizations who, in one way or another, worked with foreign aid. It had probably never happened before that the Swedish government had shown such a clear interest in radically and quickly improving another nation's social well-being and to do this through so-called NGOs (Non-Government Organizations). It is true that the government's Minister for Foreign Aid had called a meeting every now and then, but the Prime Minister taking the initiative himself was very remarkable and pleasant.

The reason for the invitation was the media's revelations about Romania's miserable situation after Ceausescu's fall.

"Everybody was there," P-O Klint, the former Chairman of Erikshjälpen's board, observed. "From our horizon, we had already taken a decision in principle to build a children's village close to the town of Oradea in the Bihor province, which borders on

---

1   The Swedish Prime Minister's offices. –*Translator's note*

Hungary to the west.

In the morning of Christmas Eve itself, our director had taken the initiative of a telephone conference call when we decided to make a real contribution to Romania in some way. The day after the conference, an astonished world witnessed the execution of the Ceausescu couple on TV," says P-O Klint.

* * *

"For a couple of years, there have been good relations with the missionaries Linda and Lars Hörnberg in Romania," says P-O Klint. "The Hörnberg's were established in Romania and we supported them with selected measures within the hospital sector. The largest contribution was the purchase of a dialysis machine for the hospital in Oradea.

At our board meeting on Christmas Eve, we decided in principle to make a real and long-term effort for the children in Romania."

* * *

Back in Romania, Linda and Lars Hörnberg were agonizing over the chaotic situation that had emerged so quickly after the removal of the Ceausescu couple. It was not only the miners and the people of the church who revealed deep destitution among the population, but also, the social authorities wrung their hands in despair, paralyzed by the hordes of children who roamed the streets or who were literally imprisoned in their upturned cots at the state institutions, apathetically rocking back and forth like animals in cages. Those responsible at the government agencies in Romania baulked at the images and were ashamed before the TV audiences in the western world. Were there no normal children in Romania, you would ask yourself as you saw the reports on TV. What was the fundamental fault with the Romanian society?

What the TV showed the world turned out to be true, but the media could not sound the depth of the tragedy.

Since Lars and Linda were in Romania, they were well-informed about the country's precarious situation, and they had known for4 along time what they wanted to do the day the possibilities would be given. Soon, they were in touch with their friends in Sweden. Several foreign aid organizations that had previously supported them in their work were not yet ready for larger efforts. When they called Erikshjälpen, there was a readiness there to make a real effort immediately for the disadvantaged children.

"Our director at Erikshjälpen reacted enthusiastically when the Hörnberg's got in touch, and the case was in that way guided in to the board, which held its board meeting on that very Christmas Eve," says P-O Klint. "Lars Hörnberg was well-known to us not least through the effort we had done after the earthquake in Armenia. When he now pleaded with us, we did not hesitate to recognize the offer for collaboration."

* * *

So this was the situation as the Prime Minister Ingvar Carlsson called a meeting in Rosenbad. The atmosphere was charged with positive expectations. To Erikshjälpen, it felt like the Swedish state was ready to make a unique and quick effort for organizations with Romania on their agendas.

"Göran Ivarsson, department manager at Erikshjälpen, accompanied me there," says P-O Klint. "He was very straightforward in his description of the Romanian state-operated children's institutions. Göran had been visiting Oradea, and as an experienced politician within the County Council of Jönköping, he could formulate his impressions in a professional way."

"How are Swedish foreign aid organizations preparing for what is now being revealed?" Göran Ivarsson asked.

To the Prime Minister Ingvar Carlsson, that question was welcome. Getting down to business quickly and tangibly, appealed to him. After all, that was why he had called a meeting. The Prime Minister wanted to know what plans the foreign aid organizations had and Göran's question came at a suitable moment.

P-O Klint added to Göran's proposal:
"We at Erikshjälpen have already taken the decision to make a contribution," said P-O Klint. "We have studied the area by ourselves and contacts with local authorities have been established. We are already in the process of building a children's village in Oradea for about 100 children. The children will have a secure upbringing, a homely environment with house parents, education and healthcare. In short, we want to provide the children with a completely normal life. We have experienced people in place and can immediately develop the human capital that is within the children."

"It felt good that we had a proposal that was well worked-out," says P-O Klint. "It felt as though we had an advance ahead of other foreign aid organizations. In fact, we already had construction up and running. It felt nice to be able to present a well worked-out and realistic project."

"Our proposal," said P-O Klint to the Prime Minister, "is that the Swedish state gives crown for crown, that is, 50 percent of the estimated cost for the effort that is now being made in Oradea."

Ingvar Carlsson's Minister for Foreign Aid, Carl Tham, was also present at the seminar at Rosenbad, and when P-O Klint proposed that the Swedish state would come up with half of the cost, he probably thought that it was time to formulate a good surprise.

"The Chairman of Erikshjälpen," said Carl Tham, "is probably well updated with the 20/80 rule for SIDA. That is, if a foreign aid organization will invest 20 percent of the cost for a project, SIDA will contribute 80 percent."

Yes, P-O knew that, but here, Erikshjälpen was not interested in the state having the economic upper hand, but wanted to satisfy with a fifty/fifty effort.

Erikshjälpen was, at that time, a people's organization, based on small and large people's economic contributions. Contributions came from children, families, Sunday schools and school classes. Most of the time, the gifts were submitted guided with intercession for the organization that wanted to and was able to administrate their gifts.

Carl Tham's words had still been spoken and were meant to be generous. P-O was very grateful, and the other delegates at the seminar were gasping deeply for breath. What a thing Tham is bringing! What a reception you get here from the representatives of the state!

But after a while, the Minister of Foreign Aid Carl Tham's remarks appeared strange, to say the least.

When Erikshjälpen's foreign aid administrator Bernt Einarsson later contacted SIDA, the response turned out to be that Romania was not included as a focus nation, and neither was Sida working with any budget for Romania.

There are to explanations to Tham putting his foot in his

mouth in such a fatal way. The first one is that he wanted to impress the seminar's participants, or he was very poorly informed of his own organization's principles.

"There was no 80 percent, as promised by Tham, then," P-O Klint says cynically. "Neither was there any 50 percent, as I had proposed. There was nothing! Not one crown from the Swedish state or from SIDA arrived for our project! Lots of promises but no money where their mouths were!

I wrote to the Prime Minister and reminded him of his wholehearted initiative and the Minister for Foreign Aid's previous promises," P-O continues.

The response did not take too long to arrive.

"Thank You for Your letter," the Prime Minister writes. "Erikshjälpen's efforts for the benefit of the Romanian children, with or without government aid, are very important /.../ for their possibilities of a future more fit for human beings /.../ I have noted that You have applied for funds for projects with SIDA. As a Minister, I can of course not have any opinions of the handling of the case as SIDA is an agency that is independent from the government," the Prime Minister concludes.

* * *

Before the meeting at Rosenbad, Erikshjälpen had thus already started building the children's village that would later be called Caminul Felix.

The construction engineer Björn Cederqvist, Falköping, had been contacted by Göran Ivarsson when grounds had been allotted by the authorities in Oradea.

In the Pentecostal congregation in Falköping, there were creative and resolute members who knew Linda and Lars Hörnberg well. Lars had been a pastor in the church. Linda had also served the congregation and brought it great joy.

When the earthquake in Armenia happened one year earlier, Lars took the initiative to rebuild several towns, and had managed to get the wholehearted support of the Soviet Union Embassy in Stockholm. Lars also had the undivided support of Erikshjälpen at that time, too. It was not only buildings that were erected in Armenia and it was not only the Pentecostal church in Falköping and Erikshjälpen that came hurrying. It was the entire European Pentecostal movement under an ad hoc committee named EPRO that backed the reconstruction work and Erikshjälpen's director was named the Småland "Citizen of the Year" in 1991 by the county's media for the speed by which the project was carried out.

The Pentecostals of Falköping had risen as one and the entire community was engaged, money was raised, professionals of both genders traveled to Armenia and made heroic efforts on a voluntary basis.

When the turn now came for Romania to get Swedish aid and support, the Pentecostal church in Falköping was ready for a second time. Once again, money and professionals were coming in to help.

Bernt Einarsson, project leader at Erikshjälpen, was willing to take over after Göran Ivarsson who realized that his capacity as the assistant director of Erikshjälpen required his efforts in other areas.

Bernt is a construction engineer and had the right contacts with architects and professionals in the Vetlanda and Huskvarna areas. Lots of skilled men and women volunteered to join in the realization of the children's village Caminul Felix.

Many things thus happened in a short time after Erikshjälpen's decision on Christmas Eve in 1989.

The Prime Minister had had his seminar at Rosenbad, with no obligations. Blueprints had been developed. Jennie's pacifier had become known, newspaper articles had been written, and millions of crowns had flooded in from individual donors and companies.

The Pentecostal church in Falköping and volunteers from Småland and Västergötland reported interest in joining. More trips to Romania were made to contact the authorities in Oradea. Where would the children's village be built? Which authority in Oradea owned land after the fall of Communism? Was there any person within the Oradea municipality whose word had an impact and whom we could trust?

"Well, there were many issues we had to deal with," says P-O Klint. "I tried ideas and thoughts on Erikshjälpen's staff. Lars Hörnberg came home with influential people from the Baptist church in Oradea. One of these was Pastor Paul Negrut, who at that time was an important person within the international Baptist union. There were rumors that he was even being considered as a leading politician in the re-born Romania, indeed perhaps even a future Presidential candidate.

But it was still on the ground in Oradea that things had to be decided," P-O Klint continues.

"I remember one of the first visits we made there. The County Governor Petru Ungur received us in Oradea's city hall. Ungur had gathered influential decision-making people in his office and on the table there was a large sketch of what they wanted to do. Even a model of a new, state-run children's institution had been set up."

"This is how we want to handle the unusual situation that has occurred," said Petru Ungur. "But we have no money to realize it."

They discussed the model and the Swedes realized that the County Governor and his friends were fundamentally completely serious.

"Welcome back tomorrow," said Petru Ungur. "Then, we will travel the area and look at possible sites for a children's village."

* * *

"Eight politicians met us the next morning," P-O Klint remembers. "Several sites were shown to us and finally we got to the place which became Caminul Felix.

But we soon noticed that there was a disturbance in the air. Yesterday's positive atmosphere had all changed. The enthusiasm from the County Governor and his men was disturbed by something, but what? Our interpreter gave us some information about where the disturbance came from."

"You have to understand that these politicians have a Communist background," said the interpreter. "They have been talking between themselves and wondered what lies behind Erikshjälpen's desire to build. It cannot only be a Humanist thought that has brought them here. There must be something else behind the interest that they are showing," the interpreter explained about their changed attitude.

"They had gone into suspicion gridlock. We had deals and agreements all written. All that remained was to sign them at lunch. But the atmosphere was tense," P-O remembers.

"Would we be able to sign the deal that both parties had desired yesterday?"

P-O thought that all hope was gone.

"Suddenly, I remembered Armenia again, and the top dignitaries from Moscow whom we had met at Roland Nelsson's home in Vetlanda. Roland and Lars Hörnberg had met several influential politicians at their visits to Moscow, who had found confidence in the way that Erikshjälpen had played its cards when reconstruction homes in Armenia. 50,000 dollars had been handed over in Yerevan, which were later on followed by more dollars and the job in Armenia was done.

Did I perhaps have the business cards with me in my wallet that I had been given by the people from Moscow at Roland Nelsson's home?" P-O thought when the tense atmosphere would not be relieved at the luncheon table. "I checked, yes, there were still there in my wallet! There was the business card of the Deputy Mayor of Moscow, Mr Menshikov! And there were other well-known names! There were also a couple of business cards from top diplomats from the Soviet Embassy in Stockholm, including the Ambassador Alexander Kudinov's. I took out the business cards while telling them about Armenia. That turned out to be dynamite to the old Communists at the luncheon table!

They started discussing among themselves. They soon understood that we were not pursuing our own interests or our own financial gain. They understood that their skepticism was unfounded. The good atmosphere from yesterday materialized immediately. The papers were brought out and we signed the deal!"

* * *

The children's village Caminul Felix had been completed! Six family houses had been erected with room for 16 children in each, plus one administration building and a large assembly hall! Now the opening would take place!

P-O got the Swedish entertainment catalog. All famous artists would of course attend the opening, and they were duly invited! The Prime Minister was invited as well! But none of these could make it.

* * *

What had happened in Oradea was unique and absolutely incredible. The children's village had been realized! Beautiful houses, painted in bright colors.

The opening took place on May 27, 1992. People came from Sweden, England, Germany, the USA. Of course, "all" influential people from Romania came. More than 1,500 people came. The Swedish Ambassador in Bucharest, Nils Rosenberg, was there representing Sweden and the Prime Minister.

The first two house parents Joan and Carmen Vese had been employed and were there with their two children of their own, David, 12, and Elisa, 10.

The first abandoned child who came "home" was little Iona Urcan, six and a half years old, who had been lying tied to her bed at a state institution somewhere in the Bihor province. When she had her first meal in the newly built children's village, she lay on the floor and lapped up her food like a small feline animal. She quickly recovered and is today a young person, a fully normal citizen of the society with schooling and education behind her. A beautiful young lady in the Romanian society.

* * *

"Caminul Felix has become a pilot project for all of Romania," says P-O Klint. "Taking into consideration that there are perhaps more than 200,000 orphans in Romania at poorly managed orphanages, even more needs to be done. In the Bihor province alone, there are more than 50,000 children, abandoned or institutionalized, according to government agency sources. Then, a project like this needs to be followed by more."

The vision that the Hörnberg's carried, was linked with donors and companies and thus, it was realized to an extent that no one has yet seen the end of.

Further on in this book, the reader will experience more of the same thing!

Chapter

7

"What I have - I give!"

The year is 1992 and Caminul Felix now lies as a perfect jewel in a raped and wounded country. It is a gift from Erikshjälpen's many donors. More than 100 children live there, children who used to be considered worthless. Now, they have been given a home, a family, self-confidence, they feel protected and are met with love that never runs dry!

The time had come to give thanks to God, time to amaze at what had happened so soon, time to focus now at how all of this unique project would meet the future in the best way.

What had begun also needed to be continued.

Linda's and Lars's hearts had been moved into commitment and God had given his blessing for their vision and the new concept of child and youth care in Romania. Now, they were standing there as responsible for a large multitude of children, responsible for their upbringing and future, household and food, clothes and schooling. They had six pairs of parents and a number of coworkers. Houses and grounds need to be taken care of. A large administration is up and running and many decisions have to be taken that cost money and staff need to be selected and taken care of. The two pioneers need plenty of friends who can support them with continued care and commitment!

As far as Erikshjälpen was concerned, this was the largest project that had ever been launched.

A little girl, Jennie from Eksjö, had set an abundant number of individual donors and Swedish companies on the track, and that had resulted in a fundraising result that had become the largest in Erikshjälpen's history. The children's village Caminul Felix was valued at 14 million crowns! The fundraising in the first months alone had risen to six million crowns. Swedish companies manufacturing wooden houses, white goods, paint and other materials contributed at minimum prices or donated what was needed. About a hundred volunteer workers from Sweden succeeded each other in the erection and completion of the village.

Linda Hörnberg and Bernt Einarsson - the groundbreaking ceremony.

At the inauguration, the entire yard in front of the administration building was filled with children and teenagers, a busload of guests from Sweden, the Swedish Ambassador from Bucharest, local authority figures, the national TV and radio, Linda and Lars Hörnberg, house parents, the children's choir that was already well-rehearsed under its enthusiastic leader Linda. A miracle, a jewel, a gift from God to Oradea, yes, to the whole nation is now standing there in all its glory.

Several voices were raised; this is fantastic, let us move on and build more similar villages in Romania! From the Baptist congregation came Gheorge Dejeu, professor of sociology. Geo was well-known throughout the country as an expert within the field and had knowledge that hardly anybody else in Romania had acquired. He and his wife became one of the first house parent couples. What an asset for the new concept that had now been initiated in the country!

The Chairman of Erikshjälpen's board, P-O Klint, was euphoric

Many attended the inauguration.

and saw before him a chain of Caminul Felix villages being built in the country. He appeared boldly on Romanian TV and media. But would Erikshjälpen manage or dare to take on further responsibility?

P-O's idea was planted in fertile ground even though Erikshjälpen did not take on new construction responsibility. But perhaps it is more important to open up the door to other enterprising people and organizations than to jealously guard the market, so to speak.

* * *

There were thus other individuals and their organizations who, just as Erikshjälpen, came to help. The rumor of what had happened had spread both to England and the U.S. The good news of a new dawning era for street kids and abandoned children was mainly conveyed by Linda and Lars who had deep connections for many years with key people in those countries.

The Swedish ambassador, Nils Rosenberg, speaks at the inauguration.

Linda had been a student at a Bible college in England where John Wildrianne was the principal.

Lars met with John in connection with Erikshjälpen and EPRO building in Armenia after the earthquake.

It was John whom I had met on different occasions, and the EPRO had been formed on his initiative. The EPRO collaborated heavily at Erikshjälpen's efforts in Romania.

John had also had Romania on his heart and visited the country every year for the last 35 years. Now, I met him again, fully committed to Hörnbergs' project. His efforts would be of great importance to the continued development of Caminul Felix!

"I have shared Linda's and Lars's vision since the beginning," says John Wildrianne. "Linda was one of our students at our Bible college in England many years ago. She was on fire for the

A little Romanian girl.

evangelization of eastern Europe. She had a wonderful singing voice and it wasn't too long until she was present at both Pentecostal and Baptist congregations in Romania, which was under control of the Communist system and Ceausescu's mismanagement.

I got to know Lars after the great earthquake in Armenia and the subsequent events," John continues, and recalls the collaboration that Erikshjälpen had with the English organization In Care, which is the Assemblies of God's aid organization in England.

"During one of my visits to Romania, I heard about Caminul Felix. I'd heard that Linda and Lars had moved from Sweden to Romania. I went to see them and they gave me even more of the vision I'd heard for many years from Linda. They were eager to show me the place where their vision would come true. That was around 1990-1991.

At a later visit to Oradea," John continues, "I saw Caminul Felix completed and it was both exciting and touching to see what

Roland Nelsson, Bernt Einarsson and P-O Klint from Erikshjälpen.

had happened. Following my visit, we decided at In Care to take responsibility as sponsors for a number of children at Caminul Felix."

* * *

Robert Pagett, the founder of Assist International in the U.S., and his wife Charlene, were pastoring a congregation with missions on its agenda. Moreover, Bob was a member of Youth With A Mission and of Rotary.

When the Berlin wall came down in 1989, Bob felt God calling him to eastern Europe. That was how he started Assist International. His organization had children and the distribution of medicines on its agenda.

That is how he came to Romania, and at his first visit, the head of the Romanian Center for Disease Control, Dr. Patrascu, met him. Dr.Patrascu had attracted a lot of attention when he, after examining a girl diagnosed with leukemia, understood that she in fact was infected with HIV. He reported this to the Minister at the Ministry of Health, who went to President Ceausescu, who responded indignantly:

"We haven't got any AIDS anywhere in this country! That's Western Europe's problem! There's no AIDS in the Communist countries!"

But soon, it emerged that AIDS was present throughout all of Romania. Dr. Patrascu was fired and his laboratory was closed.

"One single word about this and you're a dead man," were the last words before he was sent out in the cold.

It did not take many months before it was the Ceausescus who were sent to the realm of the dead instead.

Dr. Patrascu was asked by Bob to come over to the U.S. for a lecturing tour. Bob Pagett and Assist International were still completely unknown concepts in the U.S., but his guest from Romania met huge attention, and it was that way that Bob was asked by influential Americans if he could open the way for humanitarian aid to Romania.

It was that way that Bob and Charlene got the proposal to visit Caminul Felix and Linda and Lars Hörnberg.

"It became clear to us," Bob says, "that the Hörnberg's needed support for their growing work, and when the Hörnberg's asked us if we could arrange a tour in the U.S. for the children's choir from Caminul Felix, we knew what to do."

* * *

After about ten years, the second Caminul Felix (CF 2) was ready to be opened in 2001, about 10 kilometers form the first one. It was Professor Geo Dejeu who was the Master of Ceremonies at the feast where everybody had come, from England, from the U.S., Sweden and Australia, to mention a few of the countries involved in Caminul Felix 2. A large number of local and national experts within the child and youth care sector from Romania were present, and Geo was the proud host for an unequalled feast out in the broiling sunshine. There was a whole hog roast, and guests were crowding in and out of the ten newly constructed houses to inspect quality and elegance. The houses had been erected by teams from the U.S., through Assist International, England and Sweden.

England and the U.S. were now involved in a strongly growing commitment to Caminul Felix. John Wildrianne had had a flow of information about what went on in Oradea from his former student Linda Hutchens and the International Training Bible Institute in England. Several churches in England joined, and soon, Pastor Peter

Jenkins from the Amblecote Christian Centre was one of the most powerful supporters of Caminul Felix.

Peter Jenkins and Bob Pagett

Chapter
8

A mother and a father

"The idea with Caminul Felix was to provide the children with a mother and a father, a home with siblings, a safe and secure home. That is how the vision could be summed up," says Lars.

When it all once began, it was perhaps not easy for the future house parents to predict the consequences of their decisions.

"The house parents actually had to toil quite considerably to convince authorities and teachers that the abandoned children belonged to the Romanian society," says Lars. "They fought for the children's rights in all instances. Their new mothers and fathers showed courage that we are proud of! The parents at Caminul Felix are the coolest champions in the world, they take impressive responsibility for a development of society that no authority could dream of. The building blocks for these new things are the abandoned children of Romania!"

Everyone who has seen what is happening there at Caminul Felix understands that it is no leisure activity that the house parents are pursuing. The commitment is full-time, to love and to care for the entire family of children – 12-18 children. It is not always easy, but they experience that God has called them to that task.

When you get the opportunity to speak with a mother and a father, they express their love for their children, and it is no different from parents' love for their biological children.

One event at Caminul Felix recently shows how a couple of the house parents – Ghita and Radiana – reacted just as any other pair of parents would have done. One morning, the smaller children at the playground were in full swing as usual, when the door was suddenly thrown wide open and upset little voices were crying: "Mommy, Daddy, come! Aurel's been bitten by a dog!" Several of the house's siblings dashed forward, making noise and doing everything to make the matter as big as possible, jumping around the little boy who was whimpering over his injured arm. All the children were talking at once. But it soon turned out that he had

One of the first families

not been bitten, only frightened by a dog. Ghita and Radiana understood the situation at once, tried to calm the upset little chatterboxes and their exaggerated reaction. Daddy took Aurel's hand and said while explaining to everyone: "Come on now, Aurel! Let's go inside and sort things out!" He gently took the child into the house, closed the door, and with that, the commotion stayed outside. Inside the door was the good and normal atmosphere of the home. That is probably how any father would have reacted, calmly and indulgently.

The parents are key people in the concept that constitutes the idea of Caminul Felix. They are the little community's ensured future.

Of course, the parent couples are so different, but all of them are charged with special personalities and characters. Such attributes are developed clearly when they suddenly arrive at their new and untested destination.

The Puscas family

These young parent couples have not emerged from any dead-end of society where there was nothing else to do than to make their way to Caminul Felix. On the contrary, they have taken their decision after carefully considering in prayer if their decision really was God's way for their lives. They are well-educated and mature people. Several of them were in the middle of a professional career: engineers, teachers, economists, child minders, theologians, pastors, trained social workers, academics. Others were trained in hands-on jobs: carpenters, construction workers, etc.

It is important to stress these personal qualities of the house parents. It is even more important to stress their stable marriages. Some of them have children of their own or are expecting children, but all of them feel called by God to also become parents of abandoned children.

"The ideas, or, shall we say, the blueprint for how we would shape Caminul Felix, comes from other parts of the world," says Lars Hörnberg. "They come from Sweden, America, England. But

Mircea and Lidia with family.

the staff is Romanian. The administration, the family parents and the leadership is Romanian. The blueprint is from abroad, but the work is Romanian. The house parents and the staff's character is something very important to us," Lars continues. "Whoever you are, you carry your personality with you. This is important. It is of utmost importance that you are genuine as a person. You have been called by God; you have been equipped by God; you carry a heart that feels empathy and a conviction and you have decided to love the children that you have been given care of, perhaps 70 children who carry traumatic experiences with them as being unwanted and abandoned. These family parents return the children to normal conditions through love."

* * *

Shall we take a little tour and meet a few of these house parent couples, one couple that has been there from the very first moments at Caminul Felix and one couple that has come in a bit later? From the personal interviews that have been made, we have a first-hand insight into what it means to live day by day in an everyday reality that they have chosen. All couples are committed believers, they are disciples of Jesus.

We have already met one couple, Ghita and Radiana Tiplea. We will let Ghita tell his own story:

"I met God's calling already during my school days. Some of my friends at school came from a state children's home and I could often see how miserable they were. When the rest of us told them about our parents and conditions at home, they could never do the same. It was absolutely clear that they longed for what we had.

I understood already then that God was speaking to me about what they were missing in their lives. I often asked myself how I would be able to help. I really wanted them to have a home with a good atmosphere, just as I had. You know, I thought that when I grew up myself and got married, I'd open my home to lonely and abandoned children.

So then, the years went by, and I forgot what God had spoken to me about during my childhood years. I went to high school and then I was conscripted for 18 m0nths. After my military service, I was accepted at a Bible college in Oradea. I studied church music for a future mission as a pastor with music as my main task.

During my second year at school, I participated in a music camp where one of the leaders told me that God had given him a vision where he'd seen me surrounded by children. He said that God surely had called me to work among children. I was dumbfounded! Here I was planning a career as a church musician, and now God returned to me and said that he wanted me involved in children's ministry! Eventually, I graduated, after which I went my own ways and begun working in a local church."

Radiana, Ghita's wife, says that both of them come from good Christian families and that their upbringings were safe and happy. Radiana's parents died early on and their demise had a heavy impact on her life and continued education.

"One day, we met our pastor who told us about Caminul Felix," says Ghita. "He talked about the children there and the misery they had been brought out of. He told us about the desperate needs they had to get good parent couples for the children that were constantly coming in. He encouraged us to consider whether or not we were to take on such a task. He thought that we were suitable for that.

Radiana and I said that we weren't ready for such a task and that it took a certain type of training suitable for people equipped in a certain way. We said that we couldn't even consider the job. We said that we really couldn't, we didn't know anything about that. But it seemed as though he wasn't listening to what we said. Instead, he asked us to at least meet the children before we would finally make up our minds.

OK, we went there and met the children and we were immediately hooked! What we saw was that each and every single child deserved all what God could give them through us. We obeyed God's voice and in 1996, we were there as house parents!"

Radiana's gentle and pleasant explanation gives us a clear message as to why they eventually accepted the call.

"When we heard that Caminul Felix needed yet another parent couple I said no, I didn't want to! But we were still persuaded to at least go there and see. Step by step I realized their need for us. The children captivated my heart and I can say that the emotions I had for them became so strong that I couldn't tear myself away from them anymore. We used to go there every now and then as visitors and spent some hours with the children. When we wanted to go home to our place, they pleaded with us: 'Don't go, stay with us!' I said that we were coming back, but inside, I was certain that we'd never stay. Back home – no, we couldn't forget them! God had called us. Actually, it's difficult to explain this whole process.

We prayed a lot for the matter and God's guidance. Every night we dreamed about the children we'd met. The dream was always so vivid. When I woke up in the morning, I told Ghita that I'd been dreaming so and so, and Ghita said that so had he. I'd been studying to become a teacher and not only to become a parent. Becoming a teacher was my absolute highest desire. That was what prevented me from obeying God from the beginning.

The situation was untenable and finally we went out to Caminul Felix again to speak to Linda and Lars. It didn't take long until we got the reply that they had accepted us as house parents and that the door was open to us if we wanted to come.

During a three-month period as interns, we were tested, and it was a lovely time. Then, we finally became house parents and I'm convinced that that's the best choice we've made. To get to invest our lives for these children gives us joy that's difficult to describe."

Radiana is standing in her living room looking out through the window and you can hear her think out loud: "I often stand here watching the children playing outside together with the children from the other homes at Caminul Felix and I wonder: 'What would have become of them if they hadn't been saved from their humiliation and come here? Perhaps they wouldn´t been alive today.' I have never regretted my decision to become a mother to my children!"

* * *

Mircea and Lidia became one of the very first couples who came in 1992 after graduation. They have fostered 20 children together and in the year 2003, Mircea remembered:
"We came here eleven years ago. My then fiancé was working as a therapist for disabled people but when she heard about the work at Caminul Felix, she wanted to move over there. We weren't married yet at that time, but we saw each other regularly. Lidia used to be here every now and then as a volunteer and I used to come here to meet her. Suddenly, I found myself being together with the children, playing with them, talking and singing, even though it was Lidia who was the very reason why I wanted to come. I realized that I also loved the children. I was so impressed by the very approach that Caminul Felix had, how well it all worked. Caminul Felix was far from a large orphanage, it was a real family home.

I decided to find out if I could get a job here – and I did! So, already the next day, I was hired as an assistant in house No. 2. That was in 1992. Lidia was working in the neighboring house, No. 1. We got married that year and felt that we wanted to become house parents."

* * *

All mothers and fathers constantly return in their thoughts to why they chose this way of life. What is the motivation?

All over the world, men and women, young people and children are deeply affected by what they hear, see and read. The blunt and naked truth about our existence is something that none of us escapes. We are being moved with compassion and the emotions are mostly difficult to handle.

But these men and women at Caminul Felix have taken one step further – they are giving their lives to the outcast and abused children. Why?

Mircea and Lidia were both 24 years when they came in as house parents in this huge family that house No. 2 consisted of. Mircea tells us why:
"I fell in love with all these children during my visits, and I became more and more committed. I saw the contrasts between the different places and orphanages that I knew about. I saw the differences in the ways that the children developed. I remember the images from the state orphanages at the time of the revolution. Those were horrible images that we saw and I understood that we could do something much better.

Lars and Linda had come to Romania and knew the situation here well, especially the conditions that the children were subject to. They had stayed in the country because their hearts had been moved. They had really decided to give their lives for what we are seeing today as a reality, to build family homes and to give the children a mother and a father. Linda and Lars are our great examples. They are constantly working so hard and they appear to love what they are doing. That gives us inspiration to become the same. What I have learned from them and from the other leaders here, I would never have learned at any university. Caminul Felix is Life's Own University!

I learned quickly that we could perform much better here for the abandoned and disadvantaged children. We'd seen them in the state orphanages, in the streets, and in many of their dreadful homes. It was a traumatic situation. So there was nothing else to do than to step forward and help them!"

Mircea tells in an informed way about life in his large family situation. Most of his new children had been kicked out and lived fearing for their lives, without any chance of care from society. Education and healthcare were unknown concepts to these children.

How nice it is to hug!

Now, another life-endorsing situation is being offered. Here at Caminul Felix, there are children of all ages. Some of them attend school which is located a bit further away. The school bus is within the area! In each family house, there are a couple of assistants who make life for the parents easier. 20 children – that probably gives quite a lot of everyday work, laundry, cooking, keeping the smallest ones busy, making beds, changing diapers, comforting and warming the little ones!

For those who come home from school, there is homework to be done – perhaps they need help with the most difficult calculations. There is school in the morning and homework in the evening. The afternoons are being spent on sports and play. Some just rest after a hard day. But not the parents, right?

"On Sundays, we take it easier," Mircea says. "But during the weekdays, all of us in the family take every chance to learn more about what we wish to improve at. Some play the guitar or the

We have new siblings!

piano, exercise or sit by the computer. Then, of course, we have the Caminul Felix choir which rehearses every week for those who wish to sing. Others do carpentry, work at the farm or with technical things. Everyone always has something to do.

Many at Caminul Felix have become adults and now work out in society. When we entered the work, our children were between nine months and 13 years. Now, the youngest is seven months and the oldest is 21 years. Our two biological children are six and seven years old.

Every Sunday, we go to church with the children who want to come along. We don't want to force them, but we encourage them to go. We try to prioritize going to church on Sundays. The smallest ones attend Sunday school while the older ones participate as teachers in Sunday school or sing with the younger ones. Some of the children have decided to become Christians. We pray for them, of course. It is our dream that our children will

*Linda and Lars Hörnberg together with med Ionica Nagy
who today works at a travel agency.*

take the sense of family with them out into the world when they leave us," Mircea continues. "Five of our previous children now live out in society, but they regularly come home and share their future plans with us.

One of the girls wanted to travel to England and the U.S. and we could help her to do that. Another one of the girls needs support and help as she is now going to university. So we came with her to her new home and furnished it neatly and nicely. All of our children need support from us parents when they move out. They often come home to visit, we are part of their lives. Sometimes, just like all other young people, they are without money and need some. Of course we help them out. As in all other families, we are one throughout life, wherever they live."

The young house parents' responsibility and intention for the role as parents is not limited to a short time of their lives. Caminul Felix is a living organism which continuously sprouts and grows. It has turned out during the 18 years since the start that the parents take on leading roles in the new Romanian society.

Ghita Tiplea now has total responsibility for the children's village Caminul Felix I and Mircea Toca is the leader of the singing and music training and for the important and expanding welfare within and without the children's village.

The fundamental vision for Linda and Lars and the entire staff has been that the revolutionary and successful child care will spin off, not only in Romania but also in other parts of Europe. Indeed, the vision is actually for the whole world.

The parent couples could become teachers and good examples to new forms and structures. They will become ambassadors spreading a successful concept for new life for thousands of unwanted little children without hope or future.

Chapter 9

Save them – Love them!

When the tragic situation in Romania became public in 1989, it turned out that horrible and terrifying cruelty had hit at the unprotected children the hardest. The state orphanages were overcrowded with abandoned and unwanted children. Poorly trained and completely inadequate staff did not have even the most fundamental abilities to care for the masses of emaciated and under stimulated children who were at the orphanages. The state orphanages have been devoid of real possibilities to reach a minimum of the qualities that are necessary to give the children the slightest chance to grow up into responsible citizens in society.

Now, however, the Romanian state has decided to give a substantial monthly subsidy to the orphanages. The subsidy is based on the number of children that are present at the orphanages.

Just about all the conditions that are needed in order to rectify the appalling shortcomings that characterize the care for the mistreated and abandoned children are missing. An entire generation carries mental and physical scars from Ceausescu's time.

The Romanian disaster has grown into a matter of international conscience. We cannot escape the terrifying images of the abuse that the youngest generation has had to endure.

In this chapter, you will get to read eight stories without any polite euphemisms. The children in the stories have been given other names so as to protect their integrity.

* * *

"The children who come to us are of all ages," it is being told. "They are all ages. One pair of siblings is Elena and Nelutu. They lived with their mother in a neighboring village. Their father was dead. The mother was a severe alcoholic and lived in extreme destitution together with her two little children. Her situation was so difficult that she sometimes thought of selling her little ones, which she actually did one day when a pair of strangers were passing through her village. The strangers gave her a bid for the children and she sold them. One child was one year old and the other one was two.

The police soon got to know about what had happened and the couple was arrested just before they were to leave Romania. There's no doubt about it; the couple had planned to sell the children to some family in another country.

The little children were taken to a hospital nearby, and from there, they came to us," the narrator continues. "They have now been with us for eight years. They're doing fine and things are going well for them at school."

* * *

"Our youngest child, Sandra," one house parent says, "is now seven months old. Her mother was a university student and

68

unmarried. When she became pregnant, she did not want to keep her newborn baby, just like many other people in similar situations. She let the hospital take care of the little one after birth. When the baby was three days old, we were told by the staff at the hospital that she needed a home. Usually they would call us first, because they know that Caminul Felix is a good place for children, so they asked to take her.

We travelled there to see the three-day-old girl, and of course we wanted to help. We took her home with us and she is developing completely normally just like any other child."

The problem is that when children such as Sandra are being born and are then abandoned by their mothers, they are being left without proper care at the state institutions. That could mean that they do not develop normally because nobody takes any time with them, nobody plays with them or embrace them. Nobody smiles at them, they do not hear anyone laughing heartily. All of this would be normal. Most certainly, it is not normal to be left in a bed day after day without any stimuli. Usually, these children stay at the hospital for one or a few years before they are left to an orphanage from which they can be adopted.

* * *

"Florica was five years old when she came to our family," another parent says. "Now, she's thirteen. She came from one of those institutions, a house for abandoned children, and was in a dreadful situation, psychologically and emotionally. When she came to us, she could neither walk nor talk, in spite of her five years. We showered her with love and care and good food, which she of course hadn't been given at the institution. She now began to take her first steps. Things went better and better and soon she talked as well.

Florica is now thirteen years and she's so beautiful. At age five, she couldn't even walk, now, she's an excellent gymnast. Her development is incredible and we thank God. She's a very happy person, always smiling, talkative and sociable. You can't see any difference between her and a child who had a mother and a father and a family from the beginning."

* * *

"One of our sons is ten years old and he's now been with us for five months. He came from a home where both his father and mother were alcoholics. Viorel and his five brothers caught the attention of the authorities and they were scattered in different places. We don't know where his brothers went, but we know how things are with Viorel.

He is disabled, he has a club foot. His father took advantage of his disability, forced him out into the streets to beg for the daily bread for the family. One family in town had mercy on the begging boy for a few months, after which they handed him over to a hospital which finally took him to us.

Viorel is naturally talented, but in the environment he'd been living in, at homes for poor and mentally disabled children, his intellect wasn't stimulated. In the normal school environment he's now in, it turns out that he is performing very well and he's now one of the best students in his class.

In spite of his disability, he's interested in a number of activities, he plays soccer and he rides around on his bicycle. He adapts to anything and he's a happy lad. He's our son!"

* * *

Yet another parent at Caminul Felix says that they have had

three children from the same family.

"Daniela is 13 years old and her brothers are twelve and eleven. Their previous conditions at home were cruel with alcoholic parents and the authorities sent the children to us. My wife and I did think that we were a bit too young to take care of such old children. Would we ever become a mother and a father to them! Would we ever be able to understand them and would they want to accept us as their new parents?

We explained to them that we tried to understand the unusual situation. After all, they did have their biological parents, and we didn't want to replace them in any way. We suggested that we could get along as friends and peers. So, for a few days, they called us by our first names and not Mom and Dad like the rest of the children in our family. We tried to relate to them as friends. Tried to let them understand that we only wanted to be facility personnel. It actually worked, but it didn't take long until they treated us as their parents and became siblings to the other children. Now, they've been with us for one year and everything works out fine."

* * *

"We have a pair of twins at our place who were born in a hospital. After birth, the mother took the children home with her instead of leaving them at the hospital as many people do. After a day or so, she found an empty and abandoned house. She placed her twins in a basket and left them on a table in a room by the street. Of course they screamed ceaselessly, so people passing by the house noticed the screams and informed the authorities who took them back to the hospital. When they finally came to us, it turned out that they hadn't developed like other children do. They didn't talk and couldn't walk either. But love and care sped up their development normally. Today, they're nine years old and are doing fine."

"Nicoleta is one of our daughters. She came together with her sister, Lidia, who's about a year older. When they came to us as small children they were in a poor condition, so thin and translucent that they couldn't manage to stand up straight and so drowsy that they had troubles staying awake. Both of their parents were alcoholics and when Nicoleta had been born, her mother was so drunk that she hardly even noticed that she'd become a mother. We later heard that it had been like that when her big sister had been born as well.

When they came to us, the children were only skin and bone. They'd never been given nutritious food. Their only food had been some sort of liquid gruel sludge. When we tried to give them more solid food in small portions with a teaspoon, they couldn't keep it down. For some reason, their tooth buds hadn't developed. Their health was deteriorating. The doctor did what he could for them to keep the food down, but he didn't succeed either. He tried to give them vitamin injections but there was hardly any flesh to stick the needle into.

We expected them to die. But one day, we had an idea. Perhaps we would separate them for a while. That helped! Suddenly both of them responded to treatment. Don't ask us why.

Now, Nicoleta is seven years old and a wonderful girl in first class. She's healthy and happy and is doing well at school. Her sister Lidia is doing just as well. It's a miracle of God and we feel blessed to have been allowed to take care of them."

* * *

"We'd like to tell about a pair of twins who are now more than two years old. They came to us about eight months ago from a state orphanage. Their mother was an unpleasant thief, always causing fights in the streets and stealing from old people who couldn't defend themselves. It wasn't always that she escaped the police, but when she was sometimes captured, she always found a way to avoid prison after her recurrent arrests.

Romanian law says you can't be imprisoned if you're pregnant, so that's what she did. She always made sure she was pregnant, and when the child was born, she willingly and happily left her newborn child for others to take care of. Now, she had produced a pair of innocent twins. That's why they're here with us right now. It's a tragic story. She isn't the only one with such a background.

It was miserable for the twins who came to us and they were very disturbed. It wasn't easy for us either to take care of a pair of babies that we couldn't communicate with, especially considering that we already had ten children in our house. But now, they're heading towards normal behavior, they're running around everywhere, talking and being mischievous. Thank God that they were given to us! We love them and want to care for them tenderly!"

Chapter

10

Casa Minunata – The wonderful house

There are so many tragic fates of life among the smallest among us.
And yet there are children who carry an even crueler fate. Those
are the ones who were born disabled. This chapter will show how
God can speak to those who want to listen and how he prepares
the way step by step towards a meaningful mission among miserable children. Adriana Paul clearly saw that total lack of understanding and empathy for these children in Romania. And she
let herself become enraptured into a wonderful adventure which
became unique for the entire country. Casa Minunata became her
fate! Adriana grew up in Arad, a town in western Romania and
worked as a nurse, but already as a child, she really wanted to work
with children and especially get a pediatric education. After a few
years, the revolution then came, and the doors into Romania were
opened. During her education, Adriana had studied French, and
in her spare time, English. Adriana used to go to the Pentecostal
church, and there, one day she met a group of Englishmen, who
had come there with supplies. Pastor John Wildrianne was the
leader of the group, and when he realized that Adriana spoke excellent English, he invited her to interpret. Shortly before this event,

she had been ordered to report to the Communist party's central office, and was given an ultimatum there: "Stop going to church if you want to have a future in Romania." She was given that order at the end of October 1989, but one month later, it was indeed the Communists who no longer had any future! The revolution has thrown them out of office. Adriana dreamed about becoming a missionary, perhaps to Asia or Africa. But after a few years of studying at Wildrianne's Bible Institute in Sussex, England, she understood that God wanted her in her native country. John Wildrianne suggested that she visit Linda and Lars Hörnberg, but she did not think it was particularly exciting. Oradea, after all, was too close to her home town. At least God could call her to the areas near the Russian border, she complained.

The Hörnberg's hired Adriana as a nurse at Caminul Felix, but there was not too much to do there, and she was never really happy. But then, something happened. A group of people from the Lions Club in Sweden came to visit. They came to see the situa-

Adriana

tion in Romania, and had an idea about helping physically and mentally disabled children. "This seems to be my thing," Adriana pondered. "I'll never forget that day, when Casa Minunata was born as a realistic and completely feasible thought," says Adriana!

* * *

During the age of Communism in Romania, children with special needs were put in institutions where they were completely neglected, or they were hidden at home. The disabled children were considered useless and completely uninteresting to society. To the families, they were a burden that the families were ashamed of.

The Lions Club in Sweden decided to build the Casa Minunata school. The name means "The wonderful house" in English. Some 30 daycare children with physical and mental disabilities were admitted. The aim of the school is to habilitate the children so that they can be integrated into normal schools or special needs schools.

A few years later, yet another building was ready for Casa Minunata, and there, Romania's first elementary school for special needs children was started. The goal is to provide the students with elementary schooling, training for an independent life, and to prepare them for the vocational training. Many people still believe that disabled children cannot be educated.

Casa Minunata has now become a new model for training and integration into normal and special needs schools for children who need special aid. At present, there are some 70 children who are being educated at Casa Minunata. The school often gets to receive study tours, and has become a model for the entire country about how to work and see successful results with disabled children's development. Several of the children, whom nobody previously had considered, have today been able to move over to ordinary schools or special needs schools. The parents can proudly see how the children are making astonishing progress. They know longer need to hide the children, nor do they have to be ashamed of them.

The teachers at Casa Minunata have received special training, and their skills are being updated through seminars and courses. Those skills are in demand around the country, and also in neighboring countries such as Ukraine and Moldova. The Romanian government has even asked them to write a proposal for a curriculum for the state special needs school.

The schools physiotherapists are working intensely to improve the student's motor skills. They have reached good results, which means that the students have become more independent after learning to walk, eat, and dress by themselves.

Every day, the students are being fetched at their homes by the school's bus. When the day is finished, they are being bussed home again.

Casa Minunata

The classrooms have been adapted to provide a stimulating environment and to enhance the curriculum's intentions to meet the needs of every single child. Huge progress is being made emotionally, and the social ability to be able to live a rich and free life is being developed powerfully.

At Casa Minunata, there are social workers who make regular visits at the parents' homes. Most of the families are completely destitute after costly doctors' visits and care programs. The children's families are very grateful that somebody finally have started caring for their children, so that they can have the chance of a worthy and meaningful life.

On January 1, 2002, the total responsibility for the project was handed over to the Foundation Casa Minunata. The Romanian government does not provide any means or subsidies for the school's activities. The municipality of Oradea gave a symbolic sum at the start of about 3,300 SEK. In order for Casa Minunata to survive, they are completely dependent on support from people who have had Casa Minunata on their hearts.

The cost of running Casa Minunata is at 180,000 SEK per month. The school is today a so-called inclusive school, That is, open to disabled children and children without any disability. The school has become much appreciated, and many families want their non-disabled children to share the school's program and attitude to life. The prosperous families who send their children to the school pay a fee that covers one third of the school's costs. But still, the school needs 120,000 SEK per month in order to cover the remainder for the children that come from the financially weak sectors of society. That support comes from individual donors as well as from the Lions Club and churches in Sweden and from churches in the U.S. and England.

* * *

The option for the parents was to keep the children at home, But then, they would be without any help and support. There are no teachers or psychologists available, and neither is there any special government agency to ask for advice. Even though the parents in such a situation can only give the child food, clothes, and medicine, they keep the child at home.

"We noticed that if the parents kept their children at home, they became isolated from the pulse of everyday life. It wasn't only friends and relatives who turned their backs on them, even the members of their own families stopped visiting them. It was as though God had punished them in public for something dreadful that their parents have done," Adriana says.

"Ordinary people didn't want to come close to a disabled child, especially if the child had a mental disability. What would we be able to do to change the attitudes towards these children whom nobody counted on and whom people were even afraid of contacting? Something had to be done, but we didn't know what.

We have fun!

The challenge was initially a bit vague. I felt for the matter, but I was afraid. We gather together to work through all the issues that would emerge when the challenge hit us so totally. The questions just kept falling all over us. We were thinking something like this: 'If you have a non-disabled child, it is of course natural for you to send the child to school every day. Of course we also have to offer the disabled children's parents a similar possibility. We have to find a place for the children to go to, in order to return home later in the day. We started realizing that that place would be called – a school.'

The next step was to contact the city's school authorities. I told them", says Adriana," that we had the means we needed to start such a school, that I knew a bit about how it would be run, and now, we wanted the authorities to support the idea. They burst out laughing and asked scornfully what qualifications I thought I had to carry through such a project. Moreover, they said that such children are uneducable. I tried to explain to them that we wanted to try it, to stimulate the children into some sort of wakefulness in

We fish as good as anybody else!

order to find out whether there wasn't something within them to connect with after all. But I didn't get any response to my offer. Oh yes, they wanted the money, and said that they wanted to use it to build a nice school for talented children.

That was of course a sad response from the department of education, but we could only accept it. All that remained now was for me to turn directly to those parents who might want to believe in the project.

We're going to start going from door to door and tell about our wonderful idea. We're going to tell them that we have a program that will change the entire family! The family's isolation will be broken!

But oh dear, how skeptical they became, how much pain that came into light. Yes, they were actively opposed against the proposition. In fact, I wasn't welcome through the doors when I told them that I had heard from the city's doctors and psychiatrists that there were disabled children in the house and that we wanted to talk about it. Perhaps I could help them. But no, the doors closed. They saw me as a far too young and opinionated lady who would come to visit without being invited! It was actually more difficult to meet the parents' attitudes than the school authorities'. But I returned, came knocking on the doors, smiled at them and tried to win their confidence, and eventually, they softened and asked themselves: 'Why is she doing all this?'

Eventually, they understood that we had no other business than to help them. Eventually, we succeeded in motivating some families, and we opened our daycare center in October 1994 with 30 children!"

Casa Minunata had come true!

"Nowadays, people in town see Casa Minunata with a positive attitude, and understand that this was exactly the way it was supposed to happen," Adriana continues.

* * *

It was thus the Lions Club in Sweden which had originally contacted Lars Hörnberg with an offer to help starting the specific project for children. No less than 6 million crowns was given by the Lions Club to the project Casa Minunata, and they then paid for operational expenses for several years. The Swedish ambassador was present at the opening, which became a great experience. The city's school authorities felt compelled to join. They were probably astonished when they heard that Sweden's representative congratulated Oradea to the opening of a special needs school, the only one in the country so far.

The special needs school's program was presented for those who were interested. The children were to arrive every day. The

I have risen from the wheelchair!   *The playground is great!*

school would provide children and parents with all the support that could be mustered, stimulation and motivation to become integrated into the work of the school. After all, it was only a few years since Romania had gone through its revolution. But Adriana and her colleagues thought that Romania could change quickly and become a valuable part of Europe and that conditions would soon become normal. As a role model, they had Sweden, where disabled children have become part of society and become integrated into ordinary schools. Adriana was completely convinced that within only a few years, Romania would experience the same thing.

It was a good start. Disabled children were to be liberated from the institutions! They would no longer be tucked away in isolated homes! They were to come out into public life and become integrated into society!

But things would not turn out to be as simple as they had hoped! First of all, there were no state or municipal funds to access. The other part of reality was that the municipal elementary schools were not suited for the disabled, and neither were the public buildings. There were no ramps for wheelchairs and there were no elevators in any school.

Adriana and her staff of teachers decided to proceed. They had a special needs school, but now, the idea was born to build an ordinary elementary school with a professionally produced curriculum."

"We were invited to the general conference of the Lions Club in order to tell them about our vision and we were met with an overwhelming response. The conference straight away decided to build a larger building in accordance with our desire, an elementary school for 40 students. We open the school in October 1996," says Adriana.

Now, the second phase of Casa Minunata had also come true!

Today, there are 70 students and 40 staff, And the curriculum is constantly being developed. There has been a request from the Ministry of education to see the curriculum. The authorities have seen that the children they thought had a low IQ or none at all and neither could write nor read, are now managing successfully. How have they managed to do this, they wonder, and which methods have the used!?

"Well," says Adriana, "we regularly invite teachers and professors both from our own country as well as from Sweden, the U.S., and England, to give lectures and develop new methods for teaching."

Another important aspect for the school is physical training and education. Further on in this book, you will get to read about that part of the activities.

"Shall we take a look at the education first?" says Adriana. "First of all, We try to understand the emotional needs of the child. In the Romanian schools, there is no consideration whatsoever as to whether a child comes from a good home or from a home with miserable conditions. They don't ask whether or not the child has had anything to eat before arriving at school. They're only interested in what the students can achieve according to the curriculum. We start by understanding where the child is and where it comes from. Our children have always heard that they are one big mistake, an accident. The parents have constantly repeated that the children are their daily cross to bear. The child of course feels that they are useless and it becomes a difficult task to motivate them for school work. It is our duty and highest wish to treat the children with respect and love, to let them know that they are valuable to us," Adriana continues.

"I thought a lot about this in the beginning. How do we get that into the curriculum? Can we succeed with the mission to love our children? But it wasn't that difficult at all. The children are open to anyone who will give them attention and love and who sees their value. God has done great things," says Adriana.". The psychologists ask us what we've done to get this vivid contact with students. 'How have you made this girl smile? She's never done that before!'

The children show clearly that they are part of what is going on. They become so happy for every little bit of progress. When the child's emotional life has been awakened – and only then – there is focus on the curriculum.

Perhaps the child will not reach the high academic results, but the goal is for every child to achieve his or her potential and possible capacity.

But then, there is physiotherapy.

Some of the students started taking their first stumbling steps when they came to school. Others perhaps could not drag themselves across the floor, the only movements was the spastic twitches in arms and legs. Such defects can sometimes become corrected surgically or only by physical training, and the child can perhaps get onto their feet. Some children have learned to sit up. They can then train their muscles further, so that the child who for 10 to 12 years has tried to rise up and sit, can now even hold a spoon in his hand and eat by himself. That child understands what has happened and is happening! Emotional motivation is so important, just as important as understanding the background of every child.

* * *

"We have four main goals at Casa Minunata," says Adriana.

"The first is the welfare of the child. Education and training of course, but welfare.

The second is the child's own family. Much attention is given to the family. It is of vital importance that the family and the school work together. This is of course well-known since a long time in all other countries, but in Romanian schools, it is an unknown concept. Through our social program and courtesy of our teachers, The parents have become part of our plan. The parents are important to success, their struggle for survival, their joy, yes, all that happens within the family is important to the students and the school's staff in order to succeed. It isn't always easy with such participation from the child's family. After all, they have no experience being part of the professional team that their child is already part of. But they've come quite fine, and many parents testimony is that the work at Casa Minunata has changed and positively affected their lives."

The third one is society. The authorities believe that the disabled children are worthless. At a church service in the Pentecostal church in Landsbro in early December 2003, Lars Hörnberg tearfully told how some Romanian authorities view disabled children: "They're hopeless! Nothing to build on! It's foolish to believe that these children are educable!"

"Not so strange, perhaps," says Adriana," as nobody had previously seen disabled children out in society or in the market places or in the open squares. When the projects again, you always heard negative comments, and people could be extremely disturbed when such a child with its teacher came into a shop. Now, people smile at them, and acceptance is much better. Of course, it will take yet much longer, and there needs to be more changes, but one thing is certain, people know today what Casa Minunata stands for and they know where they are. The media has been of great help and is a good vehicle to reach out to the general public.

The fourth one is relations with other institutions and the ministry of education," Adriana continues. "The same ministry of education which said previously that it would become a total failure has completely changed its mind. Now, they are asking Casa Minunata to write the curriculum for them, and I have been invited to give lectures at the universities! The university students need to be educated with the new view of those disadvantaged in society that Casa Minunata is pointing at. Respect, care, and appreciation of value words that are now given room in a new way of thinking", says the principal Adriana. Many university and state school students are doing internships at Casa Minunata ahead of further studies and exams.

Adriana is not satisfied. She wants to proceed with the vision. She proposed a restaurant school! Yes, why not expand with practical education. It was now no longer appropriate to send back the youth into circumstances that risk to passivize the knowledge and insights they have achieved. The Lions Club in Sweden again took a huge decision, this time by supporting the idea of a restaurant school. Christer Fält from Örnsköldsvik became the key person and conveyor of ideas and resources. He contacted the right people with the Lions Club, and now, the school has become real! It probably will not take long until new menus are being created at the country's restaurants, composed from "The wonderful house," Casa Minunata, says Christer Fält, who took over chairmanship in 2013 after Lars Hörnberg.

Recently, there was extension with six more classrooms. Some of the youth have been hired in the school's kitchen, some training to become chefs. Other young people have been hired as assistants for children with special needs.

"Casa Minunata has been based on Christian values and it certainly isn't a second-class view, but is of the highest professionalism! We give the best we have, both academically and emotionally, and we are convinced that we strongly affect the thinking of coming generations," says Adriana with a proud voice. Adriana is right about that!

* * *

In August, 1996, Adriana was invited for a holiday in South Africa. There, she met a young man named Jaco du Plessis. It was a nice acquaintance and he took her out for a few times and said that he wanted to know more about her. He asked if she was planning to return any time to South Africa which she had hardly imagined. The acquaintance with Jaco was probably only a coincidence.

Okay, but surely he could write to her? Yes, of course he could do that, but she thought that that correspondence would soon come to an end. But there were many letters from Jaco, and he wrote regularly. Adriana responded to the letters, and gradually, they got to know each other better. Eventually, Jaco came to visit Romania for Christmas and, of course, they understood that they meant something to each other.

During Jaco's first visit at Casa Minunata, he made a special discovery. It was around Christmas and there was a huge Christmas party at the school. He noticed that the children seemed to be very happy and that they were so well taken care of, but that several of the children had difficulties in moving by themselves. He told Adriana that something could be done about it. He explained to Adriana that his profession was to make prosthetic limbs. That surprised Adriana, she had not understood that before. It was complete news because such a profession did not use to exist in Romania.

Well, of course they were now head over heels in love with each other, but here, there was something else as well that God had prepared for them. "God has brought Jaco into my life, but also into my work," says Adriana, "and I thank him for that!"

Chapter

11

Theranova

One year has passed since Jaco visited Romania for the first time. Now, it is Christmas again, and Jaco and Adriana have been married. A sister organization within Caminul Felix is being created. The newlyweds spend all their time on the new challenge at Casa Minunata.

Theranova – New Therapy – has just been established at Casa Minunata as a completely new opportunity for disabled children. Everything is now happening so fast and developing well beyond the original plans. It did not take long until Jaco had occupied Casa Minunata's garage, where he made prosthetic limbs for the children who have deformed legs

Adriana and Jacob du Plessis

or arms. He was soon contacted by the Center for Neurological Rehabilitation, which actually is quite prominent in Romania, Where people come from all over the country for treatment. That treatment does not include making prosthetic limbs, because there is no such thing in the country. On the other hand, patients are being treated with gymnastics, and physically disabled children get some training in large swimming pools.

From the Center, there was a desire to establish collaboration with Jaco, which he was more than willing to have. Now, children from large parts of the country can be reached. Jaco's training provides possibilities for the Center to continue developing various opportunities for disabled children.

The work with manufacturing aids was developing quickly.

"The concept of Theranova was born in 1999 at the garage at Casa Minunata. Originally, the space in the garage was quite sufficient. I needed to be inventive and innovative to come up with how to best manufacture and shape aids for the children I saw," says Jaco du Plessis. "But soon, the need for larger spaces grew, and I needed more assistants and technicians, so we started looking around for new premises for Theranova."

The site brought them to an old Orthodox cemetery, which was no longer used for its purpose. The graveyard was about 8,000 m², overgrown with bushes and old, torn down tombstones. The place was not a pretty sight for those who lived around it, and the authorities offered the area to whoever and wanted to take it on. The town's fathers only seem to be happy to get rid of the grounds when Lars and Jaco contacted them.

The graveyard has now become the place for new life, and apart from the Teenage House, which you read about in the next chapter, the new Theranova clinic has been erected. It is a pretty and attractive one-story red brick building. Here, there was about a dozen rooms, with top-notch equipment for manufacturing aids. Here, there are also rooms for clients' consulting rooms, and for personal consultation.

"It was an extensive project that we took on," says Jaco. "An incredible amount of paperwork was begun, but after getting all the permits, construction began in 2001. We mixed cost-effective planning, Romanian labor and experience with new construction technology. The building has a unique standard for Eastern Europe and can be compared to any other similar one in Europe.

Just imagine that we have access to Otto Bock's expertise from Germany," Jaco exclaims with a wide grin. "Otto Bock is a leader within orthopedics and the disabled. By consulting them, we have the nicest and prettiest design in the workshops, and collaboration with their clever technicians is an incredible asset to us. We can't appreciate enough their eye for which machines we need and where to place them," says Jaco.

"What a day it was when we could open our new plant in June 2002! It was a huge feast with many important decision-makers

The prosthetic workshop

invited from town. Together with sponsors and friends from Casa Minunata and from the University, and physicians from the hospitals, we experienced a great day," Jaco reminisces.

"Mr. Jim Sankey is the main sponsor together with his son, Clay. They were also present, and the latter cut the ribbon and declared Theranova open. Another very welcome guest on this day was Mr. Marcel Baeriswyl from Germany, who represented Johanniter International, which trains our technicians in modern and advanced technology. Johanniter is a large supporter both technically and financially and we believe that we can increase our professional relation with them," says Jaco.

Together with Johanniter International, Jaco and Theranova made an instant effort after the disastrous earthquake in Haiti in 2010. After the devastating hurricane that hit at the Philippines in 2013, they were quickly on the ground to help out with the competence they had acquired under Jaco's leadership.

At the opening of Theranova, the South African ambassador Andries Venter was also present together with the local authorities. He has assisted powerfully to the realization of Theranova from the beginning to the end.

Theranova today appears as the realized hope and dream for many single patients to get the help they need physically. Among them are those who have perhaps felt that they are a burden to society, but not only to society, but they also feel indebted to their families for not being able to contribute with support. Our children and teenagers who have grown up with a disability that is now permanent. Perhaps they could have been helped earlier if there only had been an opportunity then. Some of these young people have consequently also developed mental disabilities.

"In and around Oradea, there are a large number of patients

who need our service," Jaco continues. "But we always need to ask ourselves the question: 'Who or what are we to prioritize?' We have been focusing on four groups of patients:

1/ Our roots belong to the children at Casa Minunata. Many children have legs that have been permanently deformed, others whose Achilles' tendons are too short and keep them from moving freely. These children need our service and we can help them.

2/ The newly refurbished state neurological rehabilitation unit receives 180-200 children during four to six weeks. 70 percent of the children who come there need our help.

3/ Many people who have lost their mobility due to diabetes, delivery injuries or accidents come to us for help.

4/ The local hospitals with orthopedics often call us."

* * *

Theranova has a clear mission, which is to provide the highest and best levels of service. They offer international professional standards and the most credible and cost-effective program for making prosthetics. All in the best interest of the patients. At Theranova, the patients always come first. The rumor of Theranova's specialist care and knowledge has spread fast, and they have opened branches in a few other places around the country, now also with clinics in Cluj Napoca, Satu Mare and in the capital city, Bucharest.

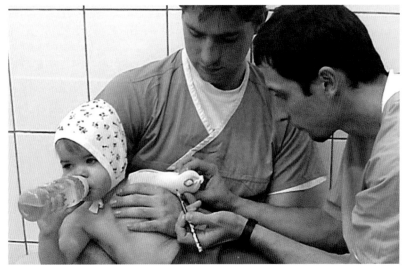

A baby gets a new arm.

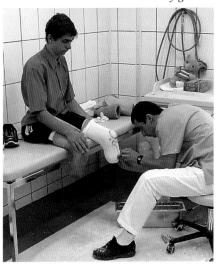

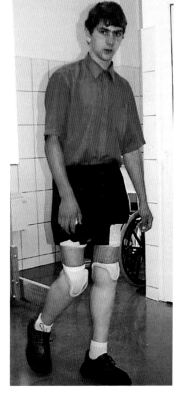

Ionel needs new legs...

...and now he can walk!

Chapter

12

The Teenage House

I felt a little stressed as I rushed down the stairs to the assembly hall on the ground floor. A colleague had said that we had visitors and I very much wanted to greet them before rushing on.

Regardless of whether or not it was necessary stress, it depended on me travelling to Romania within an hour or so together with some 30 bus travelers. It was time to open Caminul Felix.

Anyway, the sense of excitement was pulsating, I think that is a better word than stress, within my body. Imagine that we at last and so quickly had been able to build the family village Caminul Felix. Everything was a miracle by God!

We had been richly blessed by everyone who had heard about our plans to build a family village in Romania; Jennie with the pacifier, the Smålands-Tidningen daily many, many articles, single donors' money, the volunteer workers, the collaboration with the Hörnberg's. There were no flies in the ointment!

When I came down to the assembly hall, Ulla and Oliver Lindberg from Tranås were sitting there. Their visit to us was probably about a transport to eastern Europe that we were to collaborate about, I thought. We had carried out such transports of supplies of all kinds to eastern Europe ever since Poland's borders had been opened at the beginning of the 1980s.

It was fun to meet Ulla and Oliver. Their names were very well-known to me ever since the time they had been working together with Haralan Popov. Pastor Haralan, who for so many years was imprisoned in his native Bulgaria for his activities as a preacher of the Gospel. After his release, he had been extradited from his homeland, and now, Haralan travelled the West with his story of God's care in difficult circumstances. The Romanian pastor Richard Wurmbrandt had a similar experience from his homeland. The two preachers opened our eyes to the Christians' incredibly difficult ordeal behind the Iron Curtain. Ulla and Oliver Lindberg put their time and their efforts at their disposal. They arranged services in Swedish congregations for Haralan Popov. He pleaded

Oliver and Ulla

eagerly to the Swedes to pray for the imprisoned pastors in the East.

I shook Ulla's and Oliver's hands. It was very dear to me to meet them again and I told them briefly about my upcoming journey. I thought I had a lot in my bag that I could mention and about the work I was busy with right now.

But I was completely taken by surprise when Oliver asked: "Do you have any special need that you want me to pray for, Roland?"

Of course, that was a surprising question, which came already in my first conversation with them, and I did not quite know what to answer.

"You see," Oliver continued, "I'll be happy to take a tangible prayer request home with me and will pray for it during your trip to Romania."

To be completely sincere, I do not remember my answer, whether I had a tangible prayer request or not. Of course, I knew perfectly well that God hears our prayers. I had seen that many times before. But Oliver's sincere question was bewildering. After all, I had not been able to tell him about everything I wanted to, before the question came. But I think it was something about Romania that we agreed to pray for.

* * *

When you visit Oradea regularly and are being guided around by the Hörnbergs or Lisa Egerbo, there are always new things to see or experience.

Caminul Felix constantly breeds new activities. One such, to say the least, incredible activity, was that an old cemetery had been handed over to them. Caminul Felix needed yet some more space for its ministry. There were plans to build a Teenage House. In other words, a building where young people could move after their ten, twelve years at Caminul Felix. That is to say, a completely necessary measure for the youth who were now adults. They could hardly remain in the children's village. Those who had reached a working age of course needed somewhere to live. The Caminul Felix vision also comprises that complex of problems. So the municipality had referred them to a graveyard! "This is where you can build your Teenage House!"

At a first glance, it of course did not make any sense at all. Was the municipality serious? Young people who had been saved from a premature death, would they now end up in a graveyard after all?

To the Hörnberg's, there was no doubt! The graveyard would become the springboard for the Caminul Felix youth into the open society. At a visit that the Hörnberg's made in the U.S., they told about the "graveyard gift."

In the congregation, there was a group of American teenagers who listened to the story, and it did not take long until they were on site at the graveyard in Oradea. I saw them clear the brushy and bushy cemetery. They carried away old tombstones and made a respectable memorial wall out of the stones. Of course a few remaining bones were found as well. All such bones were gathered with great respect in a special place, and the place was consecrated for its purpose.

* * *

But who would finance the Teenage House? Well, that was the question.

Another building was being erected at one flank of the area.

That was the new Theranova, a prosthetic limbs workshop which had been financed by an American and which we read about in the previous chapter.

Ulla and Oliver Lindberg had been committed to Romania for several years, and especially to street children in Bucharest. They collaborated with a couple of organizations and wanted to deepen that commitment. Through their own international aid organization "People to People," they could send SEK 10,000 per month to the important labor of love. The Swedish concept for their organization is "Frälsning till Människor," "Salvation for People."

"We were fully committed to Romania when one day we met Linda and Lars Hörnberg in Aneby," said Oliver when I visited him and Ulla at their office in Tranås, an impressive establishment intended for taking the Gospel to eastern Europe.

"A good friend of ours, Alf Lindberg, had asked us to come with him," Oliver continues. "Alf would meet the Hörnberg's at Caminul Felix's Swedish office which is being led by Elise and Berndt Sanfridson. The discussion concerned teaching material that is being used in the Bible colleges in Romania and which was written by Alf Lindberg."

Ulla and Oliver listened to the discussion between Alf and the Hörnberg's at the office in Aneby. As the discussion went on, their inner beings were warmed by the attitude and personal sentiment that everybody had for the work they were committed to in Romania.

"The Hörnberg's made an enormous impression on us," says Ulla. "They seemed so upright and sincere towards those who wanted to support them in their work. From them, you could surely get feedback, as it is called in our language."

Back in Tranås, Ulla and Oliver went into their living room and their favorite armchairs at Sälggatan. Many important decisions have been taken in those armchairs. Many warm prayers have been sent up to God there.

"It was fun to meet the Hörnberg's," Ulla began. "They seemed to be the kind of people who care about their supporters. What do you think, Oliver," Ulla continued, "perhaps this is something for us?"

"I'm all with you, Ulla," Oliver replied.

For some time, Ulla and Oliver had felt that the time had come for some sort of change. Romania's needs were still weighing on their hearts, but perhaps the sluicing out of funds could continue in some other way than before.

"I actually feel peace and harmony in relation with Linda and Lars Hörnberg," Oliver continued. "If it's okay with the Hörnberg's, we'll contribute those 10,000 crowns a month that are earmarked for Romania! We'll talk to our board about it!"

The next morning, they returned to their armchairs, just as they do every morning. That is their place of prayer. That is where they read the Bible and hand the day over to the Lord's providence and guidance. It is important to the Lindberg's to be open to what God wants. The fact that things take place in that way in the Lindberg home is something that is known to everyone who supports them in their work. The donors are with them in prayer and every now and then have a request that they want Ulla and Oliver to pray for.

"When I came to the office that morning, I wrote a letter to the Hörnberg's," says Oliver. "We wanted to step forward as collaboration partners, I wrote. It was in late 1996 that the letter was written. I pointed out the importance of mutual trust. I then wrote that the feedback was of incredible importance."

"The response to the letter did not take long, and we agreed on a trustful collaboration," Ulla remembers. "As early as in January the next year, we sent the first money. That was several tens of thousands of crowns."

"We wrote in our Newsletter about our new collaboration. We published the articles that Lars Hörnberg wrote in our publications," says Ulla. "We didn't want to appear as though we were doing the writing if it was Lars who wrote. That sincerity is something, I believe, that is of great confidence-building importance. It was fun to convey the information from Romania."

* * *

When you meet Oliver at the office in Tranås, it does not take long before you still have to ask how he is doing.

"Well, I feel streams of peace and I bless you, my brother," is Oliver's usual response. "I am praying for you," he continues, and then comes the same question that I heard once a long time ago in Erikshjälpen's assembly hall: "Do you have any special need, Roland, that you want me to take in prayer?"

The reason why I still asked him about how he was doing was the knowledge that a few years ago he experienced a personal disaster that came very close to costing him his life. He was knocked unconscious in a terrible physical attack that had left its visible marks. Oliver does not move about as freely as he used to do and he takes some time when we are talking. But you do not hear him complain and there is no bitterness in his voice when he says:

"I'm waiting for God! He has promised to restore me to full health! We've never discussed anything else! We're waiting, Ulla and I, for God's intervention and we will carry on!"

It was a tough time that the family went through. What had happened had come so completely unexpected. Such an incredible event that you wonder how it could occur at all.

"We were visiting good friends in Örebro and our host, Göran, and I took some time to pursue our great favorite pastime, which was hunting," says Oliver. "Göran was then pastor of a congregation in Örebro that was doing some refurbishing work and on the way home, he just wanted to call at his working place."

"As I still had my hunting weapons in the car, I didn't want to follow him all the way into the church," says Oliver. "I wanted to keep an eye on the car outside, so I stayed in the church foyer. In the church cafeteria, there was a prayer meeting. They were praying for Örebro and the evangelism of the city. Suddenly, a complete stranger came out from the cafeteria and asked sullenly: 'Who are you and who do you think you are?'"

That is the last thing Oliver remembers before a heavy punch hit Oliver and he fell unconscious backwards onto the concrete floor. One of the culprit's accomplices continued the abuse with kicks and punches on Oliver and several ribs were broken. Breathing and heart activity stopped off and on for 15 minutes.

A despairing Göran found his friend lifeless in the church foyer and called for an ambulance. When Oliver had arrived at the hospital, Göran called Ulla, who had stayed with her good friend.

"The telephone rang and my friend handed over the receiver to me. I had a bad feeling that something wasn't right," Ulla remembers.

"Get ready and I'll come and fetch you, there's been an accident," Göran said.

"What's happened!" Ulla cried into the receiver. "Say it! I need to know!"

Ulla knew that they had been out hunting. When Göran now called and said that there had been an accident, she thought for a moment that the same thing had happened to Oliver as had happened to his father Knut a long time ago in Germany. There, his father had been killed in a tragic hunting accident.

No, it was not such an accident. Oliver had been attacked and lay unconscious in the hospital! Oliver attacked!

"It was as though life suddenly ended," says Ulla. "We'd always been out and about. We'd been travelling to Poland, Romania, the U.S. and Sweden. We constantly crisscrossed those countries during our travels for God and now... It was like driving into a mountainside. We'd always felt strong, never any sense of fatigue. God, please don't take Oliver home, we need him to remain on Earth!," Ulla cried out.

Well, it did not seem to be so terribly serious after all. Oliver woke up from his unconsciousness and probably did not have to remain in the hospital for that long.

The attack took place on a Friday night in August, and already two days later, he had been discharged, and was on his way home to Tranås! Ulla was driving. The diagnosis was concussion.

However, during the fall, things became worse with Oliver, and in December, it was really bad. He could hardly walk and neither could he talk or do anything else either. He was completely dependent on Ulla and wanted to know everything Ulla was doing. She could not leave him alone for a single hour. The doctor forbade him to travel for two years.

That was a shock to the whole of Tranås and to everyone who knew them. For more than a year, Ulla remained at Oliver's side, day and night. He needed help with everything. The burden became too great for Ulla, and after a while, she was completely exhausted.

Their son, Jörgen, returned home from his ministry as a pastor in Adelöv to assist Ulla with her work at home and in the office.

"I remember a bad day," says Ulla. "One of the people whom Oliver used to counsel called, and I stopped by the banister down to the recreation room and listened to Oliver's speech. It was, as usual, careful and slurred and barely audible. But then, suddenly, a new tone came to his voice. It became crystal clear. I understood that they were talking about spiritual things. Oliver's body was knocked out, but his spirit was alive!"

It often showed that Oliver's intellectual capacity was undamaged. The physician said that "that man is a very sick man," but when Oliver sat by the computer to write his newsletters, there was no visible quality impairment in his capacity to express himself. That was something medical science found astonishing!

"But, Oliver," I say, it must be bitter to go through such a difficult time. How do you feel about the guy who knocked you down?"

"Well, I've been told that when I was laying on the stretcher in the E.R. in Örebro, I'd said: 'Tell him from me that he is forgiven!' The perpetrator called me one week later and asked for forgiveness. I was then able to tell him personally that he was forgiven. I'm not bitter," Oliver replies.

"Have you met him afterwards," I ask.

"Yes, at two occasions during the subsequent trial."

Ulla says that she has also had an opportunity to forgive the perpetrator. When she came home after driving Oliver to the rehabilitation clinic in Jönköping and turned into the street where they live, she physically felt how bitterness wanted to grab hold of her, but by an act of will, she shut the door to that emotion! She understood purely intellectually that she needed her powers for other things than to indulge in bitterness.

"After that, I've never felt bitter," says Ulla. "We're convinced that the will to forgive has made it possible to us to move on without any bitterness in our hearts."

* * *

"For years, we have travelled in Eastern Europe and never been subject to any disturbances," Oliver says. "Our car has never been broken into. We have smuggled Bibles, but never got caught. God is the leader and I have learned to listen. What I hear God telling me gives peace in my heart. Ahead of every trip I was going to make to the East, I lay on my knees in front of the map asking God: 'Which route are we to take this time?' Every time, with 100 percent certainty, we drove straight through all borders without any problems during the Communist era."

"I remember a pastor from Romania who came visiting our office here in Tranås. We had just had 10,000 Romanian Bibles delivered to us. He was overjoyed when he saw the entire room filled with Bibles and asked if he could have one of them. 'Take as many as you want,' I replied. The pastor went and found the largest box we had and filled it with Bibles and literature. He asked me to take it with me when we travelled to Romania the next time," Oliver says.

"We were to travel to Romania together with Anton, a friend of mine, and I. We were to get through nine customs checkpoints with skilled Communist customs guys. I went on my knees in front of the map of eastern Europe and asked God which way we were to take. He showed me which one. I then called a colleague at another European mission's organization and asked whether it was wise to take the route that I'd been given certainty about. He replied that we wouldn't get any further than to the East German border!

I'd understood that I wasn't to tell Anton that I had Bibles and literature with me in the car. When we came to the first border checkpoint, the customs officers took Anton with them for a body search, but didn't show any interest in our car or the boxes with the Bibles!"

* * *

It was an exciting time that Ulla and Oliver had lived in for

Inauguration of the Teenage House. Ulla and Oliver Lindberg, Dan Butuc, Marcel Filip.

decades. When the accident had happened, perhaps many donors were wondering whether the work was over. But as they had built a prayer relation, not only a donor relation with their donors, there were now people praying for Oliver throughout the country.

The mission had grown vastly since the accident. "We have done more during these years than before," they say together!

* * *

One evening, Ulla and Oliver were visited by some good friends. They enjoyed a good meal and had a good time together, when one of the friends said in a bit of a passing way: "I've been offered 200 running meters of wall blocks with doors and windows and I don't know what to use them for. The whole lot costs 80,000 crowns and they're over at Eksjöhus." Nothing else was said about the matter that evening, and the guests thanked them for the visit and went home.

The Teenage House is now completed.

"You know, Ulla," Oliver said when they were alone, "perhaps those wall blocks could be something for Romania?"

"Yes, perhaps," Ulla replied, "call the Hörnberg's and check with them."

* * *

"Hey, Lars, do you need a house with 14 apartments," Oliver asks when he calls Lars Hörnberg in Oradea the following day.

"Eh, what are you saying, Oliver," Lars replied with a lump in his throat. "I've just come out of a prayer meeting. Our great prayer need this morning has been: 'What are we going to do with our teenagers who are now too old to stay in the children's village?' And then you're calling me asking if we need a house for teenagers! God, I'm dying with emotion," Lars cries over the phone!

"We bought the wall blocks," Oliver says. "Three jumbo tractor-trailers were loaded and drove the whole lot down there. Our organization paid the transportation cost."

Jaco du Plessis, the orthopedics maker at the adjacent Theranova, is the work leader at the Teenage House together with Romanian manpower.

"Soon it's completed," Oliver says. "Seven apartments are completed and furnished, but yet another six apartments remain before everything is finished. Of course, it costs quite a bit, but we believe that that will come in through good friends and donors."

"We needed three volunteers, carpenters, and we wrote about the need in our newsletter. Oh yes, three people from Skellefteå who did not know about each other replied and have now made a great effort this fall. They won't hesitate to go over there again," Oliver says.

* * *

As mentioned, the house is not yet completed. Every now and then there is a lack of money to complete the project. Sometimes, it has been necessary to wait for new means, and during that time, the construction work has stood still.

"I remember one day when I realized that there was now no more money accessible. I sat down in my armchair at home in Sälggatan," Oliver says. "I prayed. Suddenly, I heard myself praying: 'Now I will enter your storehouse and fetch 100,000 dollars."

Two days later, on Friday morning when they are sitting in their prayer armchairs, a lady from the U.S. calls. Ulla answered and she recognizes the lady from previous conversations, even though she rarely used to call. The woman is a prominent business owner and has won several prizes for her successful ability to run companies.

"Hi," says the woman from the U.S., "I was out on my Gold Wing motorcycle yesterday when God suddenly told me to send you 100,000 dollars. I replied that I couldn't do that, but God said that I could. The money's coming," she said. "And the money came!"

* * *

One morning, Ulla and Oliver were choosing a new book in the Bible to read from. As usual, they sat in their armchairs at home.

"This morning, I asked the Lord 'Which book do you suggest that we read from now?' As through an inner voice, I hear 'Read Jeremiah 30.' I open that book and read. When we came to the seventeenth verse, neither Ulla nor I could continue reading. To my great surprise, I saw that it said: "For I will restore health unto thee, and I will heal thee of thy wounds."

111

Soon after this incredible word that Oliver got during his prayer time, he turns on the TV and watches a show taped from a Christian channel. Benny Hinn, an American healing evangelist, is preaching. Benny Hinn usually presents healing miracles that take place during his campaigns, and now, he invites a little 7 ½-year-old girl who was born lame to come forward. She now runs forward on the TV screen and the miracle is a fact. "God hears prayer!," Oliver exclaims.

"I'm sitting there watching what God had done," says Oliver. "I'm crying with gratitude and I'm wondering how I'll be able to show my gratitude! I fall down on my knees in front of the TV as Benny Hinn says: 'Right now there's a man bending his knees in front of the TV. You've had a tragic accident that's brought balance difficulties on your left side and difficulties with coordination between your right and your left hand, and it's been said that there are symptoms of Parkinson's disease. Listen to me my brother, lay your hands against mine on the screen and I'll pray for you!' I press my hands against the TV screen and I feel God's power through my body. The physician whom I visited soon afterwards could see a visible improvement in me."

* * *

Caminul Felix became Ulla's and Oliver's new project. The commitment has given them indescribable joy. It has changed their lives!

In October, 2006, Ulla and Oliver were present when the Teenage House was to be opened. The atmosphere is intense and it is an incredibly touching moment when Oliver with great emotion thanks God for the grace to be able to be part of the ongoing miracles that take place all the time with projects connected to Caminul Felix. He calls down God's blessings over the House, and the Spirit of God touches everyone who hears Oliver's prayer.

Apart from the Teenage House at the old cemetery, Ulla and Oliver have also financed the purchase of land for Caminul Felix 2.

It is now that Assist International Assist from California first came in with their support and paid the first pump house which supplies the entire compound with water. Later a dairy was built. The Farm might be one of the best in Transylvania.

Assist International with their leaders Charlene and Bob Pagett has done an enormous impact in building up Caminul Felix Village Nr 2 with ten residential buildings. More about Assist International you will read in chapter 17.

"The donors are with us and we are happy," Ulla and Oliver Lindberg conclude.

Caminul
Felix

Village I

Caminul
Felix

CĂMINUL FELIX
ROMANIA

Village II

119

CĂMINUL FELIX VILLAGE 2

ACESTE 10 CASE AU FOST CONSTRUITE CU PARTICIPAREA MULTOR BISERICI,
OAMENI DE BINE SI CORPORATII DIN AMERICA, ANGLIA SI SUEDIA.
"ASSIST INTERNATIONAL" A FOST PARTE VITALA IN CONSTRUIREA ACESTUI COMPLEX

BYNS TIO HEM, MED FARM - OCH ADMINISTRATIONS - BIGGNADER UPPFÖRDES
MED STÖD AV AMERIKANSKA, ENGELSKA OCH SVENSKA KRISTNA FÖRSAMLINGAR
OCH FÖRETAG . "ASSIST INTERNATIONAL", CA, SAMORDNADE INSATSERNA

THESE 10 HOMES WERE BUILT WITH PARTICIPATION OF MANY CHURCHES,
INDIVIDUALS AND CORPORATIONS FROM THE U.S, U.K. AND SWEDEN.
"ASSIST INTERNATIONAL", CA, WAS A VITAL PART

Chapter

13

'Don't send me south, Lord!"'

Lisa Egerbo grew up in a home where missions had a large place. Lisa came into this world in 1953 and just as many others who grow up in an atmosphere characterized by open-mindedness and interest in countries and peoples from other parts of the world, she gave her life to God at age 16. That took place at a youth conference where Lisa met her vocation to hand over her future and service to God. Lisa still was in school, but beside her school work, she started working with the congregation's youth. Soon, she realized that that was her way. God had called and God gave his blessing.

It was in the Pentecostal church in Falköping that the friendship with Linda Hutchens emerged. Linda was already an experienced traveler to Eastern Europe, and regularly came home to Falköping with exciting tales about what it was like to work among people among other cultures.

"Linda encouraged me and the young people in the congregation to give our lives to God and to serve him," Lisa remembers. "I also wanted to do that, but I was perfectly happy at the thought of staying at home in Falköping and being involved in the youth ministry in my spare time. I was perfectly happy to get to live in Sweden!"

Linda Hutchens invited Lisa to come with her to the U.S. That was in 1977. On their way to the U.S., they stopped by England, where Linda had deep connections with the Bible College that Doreen and Jon Wildrianne ran. After all, Linda had been studying there.

"Little did I realize then what that school would mean to my future," says Lisa. "But I was so very impressed by the school's staff and their attitudes towards their students. But I had no idea that I could become one of them!"

"Anyway, we returned to Sweden after our long trip to the

Lisa Egerbo

124

U.S.," Lisa continues. "I often spoke with God about my future and asked him to show me what he wanted me to do. God's response was absolutely clear: 'You are to work full-time in your congregation in Falköping!'

Actually, that response wasn't quite what I'd expected. On my trip to England and the U.S., I had had my appetite whetted for other countries. But the response from God was clear and I stayed in my congregation in Falköping for almost eight years. Meanwhile, Linda and Lars Hörnberg were working in the same church."

Eventually, the time came for Linda and Lars to move on, and as expected, it was Romania which became their new home. Lisa kept in touch with the Hörnbergs and became the link between them and the congregation. As Lisa says herself: "I became the Hörnbergs' agent in Sweden!" in that way, Lisa was introduced and involved in the work in Romania.

Lisa together with housewifes.

"Suddenly, as a bolt out of the blue, one day I got a fax message from Lars: 'Lisa, come over here and help us!' No, no, he can't be serious, I thought. But Lars returned with his question and I couldn't escape it and I took God to heart and answered 'yes'," Lisa says.

Lars Hörnberg not only called for Lisa, he also undertook the responsibility to speak to the congregation in Falköping about pay and other social benefits for Lisa. The congregation was in on the idea and Lisa became a missionary to Romania.

"My heart was filled with such peace, because now, I understood that all of it was God's way for me. I'd now reached the age of 40 and the congregation surprised me with an enormous birthday party. Linda came all the way from Romania, and Adriana Paul also came with her. All of it seemed to be confirmation that everything was going my way," Lisa says.

The Choir sings in the Castle church, Stockholm.

The leadership in the Pentecostal church in Falköping acted wisely. They asked Lisa to make a '"test trip" to Romania. It was in February, and then, the winter weather in Romania is bad, cold and with snow and rain that just pours down. Such weather is completely depressing to many people who visit the country. That is also how it was to Lisa. She did not like the situation and longed to get back to Sweden, as soon as possible. At the end of the "test trip", she prayed sincerely: "Please Lord, I don't want to go to Romania. Please make the elders in Falköping say 'no' and that they can't manage it financially."

However, the elders did not say "no", at Lisa's huge dismay. They called her and said that everything was ready. Desperately, she said okay, but only for one year to begin with!

So, Lisa quit her ministry as a youth leader in church, sold her furniture and on April 1, 1994, she flew to Budapest, Hungary, in

The Caminul Felix Choir on tour in the Swedish arcipelago between Hönö and Styrsö. The Captain is Alvar Christensson.

order to continue by car to Oradea, Romania.

"When the decision had been taken and the journey to Romania had begun, I had peace in my soul," says Lisa. "After all, it felt real. I was going to meet a new culture and lifestyle, but still, Oradea was God's place for me!"

* * *

Lisa is one of the most important people within the leadership at Caminul Felix. Her workload is tough and great. Lisa's sense of humor and spontaneity balances everyday life and her work among her coworkers. "Don't forget," Lisa often reminds both God and the rest of us, "that Romania was opened up to me on April 1!"

Ana works for Sunflower Design.

That date suited Lisa and her happy attitude well!

Lisa's work is multi-faceted, to say the least! She is the administrator of the entire, widespread Caminul Felix organization, and together with Eli Filip, she is responsible for the sponsor system. She also finds time to teach at the Bible College in Oradea when she is not organizing the children's choir trips to Sweden and other countries.

She participates in the municipality's social functions, visit hospitals, in short, she is everywhere where people need her. Not least, she teaches teenage girls needlework, cooking and domestic skills, all in order for them to become as self-supporting as possible for the future.

Sunflower Design is Lisa's vision and initiative. Needlework such as clothes and other textiles are being made for sale. Ana, one of the first children who came to Caminul Felix, used to work here together with three other hired girls during the construction phase. A fourth girl, Adina, worked part-time, and in her spare time, she studied corporate activities at the university. Her goal was to become responsible for Sunflower Design after that. All the girls who have been hired by Lisa have been saved from the slums and grown up in loving families at Caminul Felix instead.

After a few years, Ana moved to the Bible College in England where Lisa once studied. Adina also nowadays lives in England. Five girls are employed by Sunflower Design today, and the management group consists both of Romanian and of Swedish leaders. Catarina Nilsson from Mölndal is one of them.

Lisa's initiative for Sunflower Design is an important part of the development that Caminul Felix is in. It is one of the many initiatives where each of them is designed to save and protect abandoned children for the time being and for the future.

In this book's later chapters about Thailand, you will meet Lisa in a new and exciting career as a project manager for Felix Family Village in Surat Thani.

Chapter

14

Under attack!

Successful activities sooner or later encounter various kinds of adversity. That is how it always has been and that is how it will remain. This is especially true for a project that has a pronounced Christian profile, or, as you say in evangelical church movements, God's work. Nobody should really be surprised that that happens. It happens in our own country as well as in the countries where we pursue missions. When adversity comes from among ourselves, the element of surprise becomes harder to deal with. However, the experience is that such adversity leads to new success. That has been proven throughout the human history.

Of course, this also happened to Caminul Felix. Two general attacks came suddenly after each other. Caminul Felix was actually shaken to its foundations and the adversaries were strong. I will let Lars Hörnberg tell the story by himself:

"The most difficult thing that happened in our efforts to provide the abandoned and exposed children a future was that we had a group of trustees who had actually never become part of the activities. They had never contributed anything, neither with operational costs nor spiritually speaking. Suddenly, they arrived and demanded that Caminul Felix would change its goals in favor of their own interests.

We stood up as one, house parents and missionaries, and declared that Caminul Felix was a gift to the abandoned children that we had been given the confidence to care for during five whole years, and that that is the way it will stay. These houses are their homes. Their parents are here and they live together with the children, love them and we will defend the task that we have been given. We will defend this ministry with the entire honor we can muster. We give our lives for our children!

Our adversaries were stronger than we perhaps had thought and the whole matter was taken to court and the matter became a lengthy one, for three full years. That was the most devastating process that I have ever seen. It was a terrible experience to lose fellowship with those who were among my closest friends in Oradea. The most untrue and unreasonable judgments were passed on the men and women who gave their lives for the benefit of the children. Everything suddenly became so negative.

We all stood together during these three years of accusations and demands. Our case was first tried on a local level, later to be taken all the way to the Supreme Court. We won our case and are very grateful that we came through this incredible trial without any scandals whatsoever. The children and we won our great victory together and Caminul Felix was saved. The large donation that Caminul Felix had been given by donors with warm hearts, thousands of people who had experienced that God had shown them how their money had been transformed into a unique family village, was saved. The verdict by the Supreme Court was definite.

Today, we have peace and quiet to be able to work at Caminul Felix. The good atmosphere has returned to stay, and we know that our mission is to focus on shaping our children into becoming good citizens, to provide Caminul Felix with an environment of safety and care," Lars Hörnberg finishes.

The chairman of the International Board for Caminul Felix, Bob Pagett, remembers the events with a shiver:

"All of a sudden, there were problems in the relations with the local leaders of the congregation in Oradea. Lars felt alone and isolated. At that time, he didn't have any representative board for all the organizations who shared the vision and the project. At a meeting in Sweden, a board was formed, and I was elected its chairman. The board members were elected from Sweden, England and the U.S.

Unfortunately, the problems with the board of the local congregation in Oradea became deeper, and their leaders called a meeting in Oradea. Those who were invited, however, were only Linda and Lars and myself. Those who had summoned us to the meeting simply announced that there was nothing to talk about and just handed over a letter and then the meeting was finished!

The letter that was handed over meant that Linda and Lars Hörnberg were fired. The vision that the Hörnberg's had birthed and realized and raised funds for was torpedoed by the leaders of the denomination that they had good fellowship with. The Hörnberg's were fired from their lifework! When we came back home to the Hörnberg's, it was like coming home from a funeral. We didn't know what to do.

There we were in our despair. It seemed as though Caminul Felix had been lost. All was dark and all energy was depleted. But that's when a new idea takes form. 'We'll build a new Caminul Felix! We'll build a new village, but with a farm! If things really end up so badly that we lose Caminul Felix No. 1 – as was our adversaries' goal – we can then move over to the new Caminul Felix, the one with a farm!'

During the time we were having the plans to build a new Caminul Felix – which we also did – the Court's verdict came, saying that the coup-like confiscation of Caminul Felix had been declared null and void and that the director Lars Hörnberg should be reinstalled into his position! We had won the lawsuit! But the whole matter took three years! Three years of darkness and despair.

We now have two children's villages and twice as many children in our care, and, on top of that, much else on our program. After these setbacks and crises, we have seen a remarkable development. What we have seen is nothing that any person can take the glory for – God is the only one who should be thanked!

Most of all, we'd like to forget about this whole lengthy lawsuit, but we cannot. It remains in our consciousness and it caused so much pain and stress for all of us that it needs to be told for that reason," Bob Pagett finishes.

* * *

Out of the crisis, an array of new projects was born, and the work was expanded rapidly. Action Felix was formed – the story of which will be told in another chapter – and the board of Caminul Felix was expanded with several Romanian members. One of these new board members is the attorney Ovidiu Costea, with whose help the lawsuit about Caminul Felix was won. Ovidiu is a precious and respected member of the board. He has done far more for Caminul Felix than what can be expected from a professional counselor.

* * *

The crisis at Caminul Felix had hardly been finished before a new one emerged. This time, it was the Erikshjälpen foundation, which had been the inspirer and financier of Caminul Felix 1, which participated in it. Unfortunately, that crisis too belongs to the story of success and adversities in a work of God. The story is painful to everyone who has participated actively in the fantastic story of Caminul Felix – also to individual employees and responsible people within the foundation. Therefore, my description is characterized by what happened.

The fact that the foundation is no longer involved in Caminul Felix is more than painful. The family village appeared to all as a remarkable project. It had been presented in Swedish media as a unique initiative. Individuals and associations of various kinds had raised money and furnishings, companies had dumped prices or donated equipment, a little Jennie had given her pacifier to the weeping children of Romania, hundreds of voluntary workers had travelled to Romania, built houses, painted and fixed, the Swedish Prime Minister was impressed, Romanian authorities considered Caminul Felix groundbreaking. Caminul Felix was on Romanian TV almost every week. A farm was set up that was considered the best in Transylvania. Other countries jealously saw what was happening and wanted to have the same concept. Every month, hundreds of families in Sweden sent their sponsor money to Caminul Felix, which someone had called Life's Own University. There were advanced plans to build an Academy for educating staff from all over Europe – and then all of a sudden, the foundation withdrew! The run-up to the foundation's exit was a sad and regrettable coincidence – a young woman's report from a week-long first visit to Caminul Felix and to Romania.

I do not wish to discuss in detail how the young woman's report came into being and why the foundation asked her to do it. But she fell into the same pit as many others fall into when they, after a short visit to a foreign country, give their "professional" view of a construction work in progress. The fact that the report would constitute a dissertation at a university in southern Sweden does not make things much better. Her professor at the university later regretted what had happened, as did an expert within medical science. The international criticism of the dissertation was massive. The fact that the woman in question first of all sent her report to Sweden's National Board of Health and Welfare, and, on top of that, to a number of external Swedish foreign aid organizations for assessment before presenting it to those concerned, does not make things much better. The result was dreadful; the foundation withdrew and Caminul Felix lost the sponsors who sent their sponsor money through Erikshjälpen. They had been given the impression that Caminul Felix no longer needed their money. That meant that one fourth of the support, or 25,000 crowns per month, stopped coming in.

* * *

Luckily, there was a large number of other sponsors who had joined over the years, and who sent their money to Caminul Felix through the Pentecostal church in Aneby. It was Pastor Sven Larqvist who, together with the congregation and the missionaries to Argentina, Gunnel and Lennart Englund, had formed the foundation Mi Casita (My Little House) and who had the energy and time to extend their commitment to Caminul Felix as well. Mi Casita later was transferred into becoming a part of Svenska Barnhjälpen (The Swedish Children's Aid) which had been formed by Elise and Berndt Sanfridson, former missionaries to Bangladesh and Thailand. I will return to Elise and Berndt in the chapter "Sponsor". Some of the former sponsors found their way back to Caminul Felix in that way.

Chapter

15

Action Felix

Suddenly, he was there, Jesper Hörnberg.

He had appeared every now and then in my consciousness. Sometimes, I had been asking for him. Bosse and Ulla Hörnberg, Jesper's grandparents, could spontaneously tell me about him. I met Jesper's mother sometimes and wondered where he was. We all knew, of course, how things were. Jesper's father and mother had gone their separate ways a long time ago. Those things happen, even in pastors' families. There is much breaking and twisting in our modern society and the Christian congregation inexorably sooner or later also will mirror that.

Now he was suddenly there, Jesper Hörnberg. He was with us at our board meeting. I was impressed by his ability to sketch out the future of the new things happening within Caminul Felix. In an academic and professional language, he formulated development plans for business activities that would eventually decrease the dependence of foreign capital. The income from the farm, the dairy, trading activities of different kinds would be able to ease the agony for Linda and Lars to have to ponder daily on how to be able to motivate more donors in Sweden, the U.S. and England to give their sponsor money and other support.

The way to a lasting and developing mission's project has traditionally been that it should be implemented into the visiting country's interests and then be handed over to national leadership and responsibility. The mission is a guest and not an owner. This is how we have always been reasoning in mission contexts, but the truth is that the missionaries have not always succeeded with that. At least, it has taken an unreasonably long time to hand over money-consuming projects to the nation that the mission is guesting.

But, dear reader, the old recipe that the mission should make itself superfluous in Romania perhaps should be considered from another point of view. During one of my many visits to Africa, I once met the Pentecostal movement's leaders in Burundi. They expressed their thoughts – or should I perhaps call it frustration – that the Swedish missionaries had withdrawn when the country had now ended up in devastating ethnic conflicts. "In the old days, in the 30s, when Sweden actually did not have the economic qualifications, we still had many missionaries here in Burundi," they said, "but when you have now become prosperous in Sweden, you are withdrawing, at the same time as Catholics and Jehovah's Witnesses are being sent here in large groups as missionaries. Why can't you stay with us as brothers and sisters? The international brotherhood and relations is something you have kept with other, Western countries' congregations. If you and we are no longer to associate as 'parents and children,' then can't we live together as siblings?"

When I listened to Jesper's line of reasoning, I sensed that there was something radically new in his presentation that could be compared with what I had heard in Burundi. Of course, there were no thoughts that the international aid for Romania would cease. The sponsor money was needed and will be expanded. Not only because the money is important to the recipients, but important also for the donors' own sake. The Swedes have a need to share. Giving is not only a hallmark for the Swedes, but constitute the foundation of a cultural and spiritual richness for their own country and for the individual citizen.

Jesper understood this, but he probably had yet another angle to the relation between Romania and the rest of Europe. The internationalization and cross-border reality had come to stay. After all, Romania was to become a member of the EU in 2007. If Romania could build bridges to the rest of Europe and do that on the Caminul Felix concept, it would do the country good. Caminul Felix was after all on its way to show that it was about to create the best farming in Transylvania. The new dairy would soon be finished, milk and cheese would be distributed not only to Oradea but to schools and hotels far beyond the city limits. At the old graveyard, one of Europe's best prosthetic limb workshops was now situated, Theranova. There were blueprints for advanced plans to build an Academy for educating social workers from all over Europe. Caminul Felix had indeed become a concept in Romania!

Would Caminul Felix pursue commercial activities? Of course not. The new organization Action Felix would do that, and would do it on an international experience base. Jesper knew how that should be done.

"After my parents' divorce, I moved as a relatively young man to London and spent my time studying psychology and business management, later to go and live in Oradea and join the team at Caminul Felix," Jesper says. "Caminul Felix 2 was then under construction, and I immediately felt that this is where I belong. For several years, we discussed what Action Felix was to be like, and it is now developing very well. Marcel Filip is our director and he is helped by a number of advisors from the U.S. and Europe together with Romanian staff. Marcel works in good spirit with the Romanian authorities," Jesper Hörnberg informs me.

* * *

Jesper Hörnberg is an assistant and inspirer to Marcel Filip, the director of Action Felix. They are inseparable and understand each other well.

Marcel Filip tells us:
"I trained as a mechanical engineer and worked for a few years on the open market here in Oradea. I married Eli in 1990 and

Jesper Hörnberg and Marcel Filip

after a few years, I moved with my family to Caminul Felix. I used to say that it was God who forced us there. With my basic education, I soon grew into the various tasks. Apart from my most important task as a house father and responsible for 17 children, apart from my own children, I assumed responsibility as head of construction for the new family village. Roads were to be built and maintenance of all buildings took its time. We were to build the farm and a dairy. A number of construction teams with 15 men in each came from the U.S., England and Sweden. The teams used to stay for two weeks and my task was to introduce and wrap up their two-week engagement. Ten residential houses were built in a short time. I am happy with this work. My wife likes it too! After a short while as a house father and some indoors work, she exclaimed one day: "Get out and get useful!" And I have done that – and I am doing that!

I had grown up in Romania, and when the revolution came in 1989, I was 25 years old. Soon after the revolution, I visited Sweden and the U.S. and realized that Communism had taken all my 25 years away from me. Everything was so different and well-planned in the West compared with my Communist homeland. Socially and economically, the West was so much better, even though our congregations in Romania were strong, spiritually speaking. But I was born an optimist and I thought that Romania would catch up in five years! Now, I see that I was a bit too optimistic. But this is where I will live and this is where I will die!

My personality is such that I want to get things done quickly. I like new ideas and do not want to grind on in the same style for 50 years! The Communist era is passé. I like thinking in new ways, to receive new visions and materialize them. All in the best interest of the future of the children at, and after, Caminul Felix.

My wife Eli and I now have children who have finished their basic education and are ready to step out into society.

Unemployment is high in Romania, and therefore, we will have to think carefully about how to be able to shape the future for our children. For the next ten years, we will have one hundred children from Caminul Felix who are to be integrated into the Romanian society. That forces us to find new initiatives that can create job opportunities.

Lars Hörnberg understood that the huge workload required more staff, and soon I got invaluable help from Emil Puscas, a qualified lad who, together with Paul Luncan, is lifting a giant burden from my shoulders. I have learned to delegate tasks, even if the burden to raise the means for wages is onerous.

God gave me the task, I had no choice! If I would be put before the same choice as then, I would not have any options. I am happy! Perhaps I once thought that I would become a pastor, and therefore, I studied theology. I took part in the congregation's work in my church and I loved it. But all the time, I asked for God's continued guidance, and what he wanted me to do. It is more than a

Paul Luncan, Marcel Filip and Emil Puscas.

dream to get to work with children at Caminul Felix. This is where I am and I am happy for it!"

* * *

When Jesper Hörnberg joined the work, the plans for Caminul Felix 2 had soon been realized. The attacks from the previously cooperating Romanian congregations were the reason why Caminul Felix 2 was built. The attack had seemed completely incomprehensible and unnecessary and caused so much pain, sleepless nights and court proceedings. At the worst moments, Linda and Lars thought that all that had been built was on its way to be ruined. But when the night is at its darkest, the dawn of a new day is at its closest.

* * *

At Caminul Felix, there were potential, well-qualified co-workers. The house father Marcel Filip was the kind of man who could widen his horizon and give his muscles satisfactory tasks. In London, there was Jesper Hörnberg, well-educated and prepared. The pieces of the jigsaw had been created by God, and one after another was falling into place!

* * *

Caminul Felix 2 is growing like mad, and new projects are being added all the time. Here, we have the farm with 400 cows, which is the best in Transylvania according to independent experts. Here, we have a dairy making cheese. Here, we have Sunflower Design and the Noble Hotel, which generate money for poor families and income for Caminul Felix. Here, we have a dentist's office. Every single project is being created in order to provide more abandoned children with a future and possibilities for studies and professional training.

Chapter
16

The Farm

Oftentimes, the old Pentecostal Nestor, Pastor Lewi Pethrus, is being quoted: "Everything that has life grows and develops…"

Who is surprised? That is, of course, not only the experience of a Christian. That lies within the natural laws themselves and is experienced in all life; day after night, sunshine after rain, order after chaos, life after death.

Caminul Felix is no exception from that rule.

Only a few years after the opening of Caminul Felix, the management group saw the need for the children's education. Perhaps there was no primary need for any advanced academic education, but instead, a hands-on one and at a vocational level; sewing for the girls and carpentry and mechanics for the boys.

The thoughts of a farm grew stronger and stronger.

Lars Hörnberg turned to Marcel Filip who had started looking around for a place to develop a farm. He realized that ahead of him lay an incredible challenge which required a considerable effort. Fining a piece of land would only be the beginning, then, buildings and workshops were to be erected, and after that… well, much else needed to happen.

After a lengthy search, Oradea's mayor offered a piece of land on condition that the owner of the land approved.

Oh yes, the landowner and Marcel agreed, and the work was begun at the 220 hectares, 20 of which were acquired straight away. Four cows were purchased, and when one of the cows died, one fourth of the investments thus disappeared! Marcel was thinking grim thoughts: "I'm an engineer and this is nothing for me!"

The farm obviously required quite a lot of knowledge that nobody at Caminul Felix had. But God touched a married couple

Wiew of Caminul Felix 2 oand the farm.

in the U.S., Sue and Clark Phillips, both in their 60s. They sold off their belongings in the U.S. and moved to Romania and promised to give five years to build a farm of the professional standard that they had achieved during many years in their profession. The barn for 200 cows had just been constructed by a team of 61 persons that Assist International brought to Caminul Felix. They thus made a considerable investment at the very beginning. A few years on, they have twice as many cows and the farm is recognized as the best in Transylvania. The Romanian Ministry of Health has honored them with a diploma as the best milk producer with the highest quality.

The farm has been realized through donations and gifts from the most diverse places: The Full Gospel Tabernacle, Orchard Park in the New York state, The Fellowship of Christian Farmers International, Kiwanis Fellowship and Heifer Project International. In addition, a wide array of other congregations, organizations and single donors in a number of countries.

The cowshed

The idea with the farm is to produce milk and other dairy products for orphanages around the country. But also to be able to sell the products on the open market in order to cover the farm's expenses and also to get a surplus which can contribute to cover the family villages' needs.

Apart from the production of dairy goods, they also cover the need for meat products for the family villages. They have also invested in pig and chicken breeding.

When Lars Hörnberg in the initial stage shared his vision with Marcel Filip, he expressed the opinion which you could say is dominant for the whole of Caminul Felix: "There is no return, we are moving on and will do so with God's help – yes, we want to!"

* * *

Making cheese and other dairy products go together with the

Exhibition of materials at Noble House.

milk production. Foster Farms in California has accepted the task to build and equip a plant for this. Foster Farms is one of the largest and most successful companies within its line of business in the U.S. and its participation must be considered to be of incredible value, not only for Caminul Felix but for the entire country. Foster Farms generously shares its experience and knowledge with the growing farm at Caminul Felix 2.

The farm's staff is completely Romanian, but they have a wide open door to expertise that every now and then arrives from the U.S.

* * *

In the Farm's area, Sunflower Design, started by Lisa Egerbo, is also situated. In a newly constructed building, financed by the Second Hand shop "Öppen Hand" ("Open Hand") in Nyköping, clothes and other details with a strong power of attraction are

Richard Sheppard from England, and Csaby are renovating furniture.

being produced. These products attract customers from near and from afar. Some of the products are being sold abroad when the children's choir visits the U.S., England or Sweden on their singing tours. Of course, the production contributes to the activities' costs and provides a hands-on education for many of the children and youngsters who grow up within Caminul Felix.

* * *

Noble House was, during Linda Hörnberg's time, a unique attraction which everybody had to visit when arriving at Oradea, attractive, artistically and professionally shaped by Linda's hands. If Linda was nearby when you asked a question about one thing or another, you got a very comprehensive answer. Full of inspiration, Linda told about old things – "junkyards!" – which her good friend and colleague Lisa Egerbo jokingly used to say. Linda had an eye for such things that no one else saw the value of – just as Jesus has with us sinners! Quite a number of things that used to be completely useless underwent their glorious transformation in Linda's hands, and now decorate Romanian, American or European homes. Antiques and arts attracted the visitors' interest.

Noble House's activities ceased when Linda passed away in August 2005. Instead, that building has been turned into a guest house, fully modern and comparable with any other similar facility in Oradea, where guests from nearly all the world can spend their days while studying the various parts of Caminul Felix's growing influence on the Romanian society.

Dental clinic

A few years ago, Linda and Lars visited Australia. Among the many good friends they met were the dentist Roland Gardiner and his wife Eva. A set of dental equipment was handed over to the Hörnberg's together with a promise that if there was a building in

Oradea suitable for a clinic, then the Gardiners would come over together with their sons to install the equipment. Their desire was that the equipment would serve the inhabitants of the children's villages but also other abandoned children.

A building was found and Roland and his family kept their promise and the clinic is now fully operational, with Romanian dentists and nurses. The people of the children's villages have good dental status and they also offer dental care for impoverished friends around Oradea.

Vocational School

My friend, Kurt Linner, called me one evening a few years ago. He said, "Now, I am anxious to know, Can you put my machines at a great place?"

Of course, we can, I said. In Oradea we had both space and interest in expanding the already started Flower Design for girls with Lisa Egerbo as a principal at the family villages at Caminul Felix.

Well, I did not think of the girls when Kurt Linnér offered his machines. The guys at Caminul Felix could certainly get enjoyment out of peeling, jig saw, chisel, circular saw, as well as all such equipment. Kurt had an interest in woodworking with the equipment he had in his garage in Växjö.

We started remodeling an old shed at Caminul Felix 2 and put the woodshop machines there. The ugly shed was changed into a beautiful building next to the workshop that was already running with Vasile Ardelean as boss. The new building was paid for by Kurt Linnér and his wife Birgitta. It was an expensive project.

Sometime later Kurt called again and wondered if there were

plans to start up a teaching school of woodwork, much like what we have in the Swedish secondary school. He said that if the idea would take root he was prepared to fund such training provided that a knowledgeable person wanted to go into the task as the principal, either on site in Oradea or remotely responsible

With Kurt's suggestion of a woodworking school came his promise that he was ready to finance it all. I thought about it for many minutes then my wife Gudrun, who listened to my phone call, suggested that we check with Rune Solid. In the same minute I called Rune and informed him of both Kurt's thoughts and his offer.

A few minutes later, it was clear. I told Kurt Linnér that there was a good friend of ours who had been headmaster for many years in the Secondary School who was willing to undertake the responsibility.

The rest is history, as they say, at least partly history. Everything came into place, a large number of working benches and hand tools and a scheduled curriculum was presented. Vasile and some guys from the carpentry shop went to Sweden for a week trying to understand what Rune Solid had in mind.

This Woodworking Vocational school at Caminul Felix is the first of its kind in Romania and Rune Solid is pushing for it to be a prototype for the Romanian primary school. However, if our vocational school can turn into a prototype for the Primary Romanian School and attract Romanian school authorities, our staff must get further additional training. That does not seem to trouble Rune Solid. He has already presented a 10-year plan with an academic education at the High School level for a team selected by the Executive Board for Caminul Felix.

Vasili and Rune at the Inauguration.

Children at work.

Chapter
17

Caminul Felix 2

You have already read on a number of occasions that there are two children's villages: Caminul Felix 1, which is in the municipality of San Martin, and the other children's village, Caminul Felix 2, which is a few kilometers out of town on the other side of Oradea in the Santandrei municipality.

Together, the two family villages have about 250 children and 16 parent couples.

Caminul Felix 2 came about when there was an imminent threat that the first children's village would leave them. If that had happened where would you find new homes for one hundred children who, after five years, had leaned a new way of life? That is why the second children's village was built.

Caminul Felix 2 was built out by the Farm. A piece of land had already been bought, but who and which ones would or wanted to finance a new children's village? It was a matter of millions and millions of dollars. But the people who had previously trusted God's interest in the future of abandoned children probably suspected that things would turn out well. God can wake up new donors! The hundred children who had already been given a home were of course only a small, small unit of all the thousands of abandoned children who existed in Oradea alone.

But there was land available, plenty of land!

Enter, then, "Assist International" with their leaders, Charlene and Bob Pagett from the U.S., who both invested all of their might and time into this new and extensive vision. It can be said plainly, that without the financial commitment and the strong motivation that Mr. and Mrs. Pagett planted in different congregations in the U.S., this new project would never have got off the ground.

Incredibly extensive work lay ahead. Getting all the different authorities' permits, producing blueprints and structures for what

Lars and Linda together with Charlene and Bob.

the houses would look like, finding qualified manpower, well, it took its time and plenty of energy. But, to an outside observer, this happened at the speed of lightning.

Ten new homes were to be built whose capacity would be compared to Caminul Felix 1. That also happened. Each home was financed by some congregation or groups of congregations. Many teams of workers came over from the U.S. They took time off their ordinary jobs, paid their own trips and their daily bread. They invested their lives for the nameless and innumerable multitudes of homeless and abandoned children, for the children who had already been saved, but also for those who had not yet shown their faces.

From the U.S., eight teams came and built a house each. From England, a team came that built a house, and from Falköping came a team and built "Villa Falköping".

"Villa Falköping" cost about one million Swedish crowns – which also each and every one of the other houses cost. The Falköping villa was erected with monetary means that had been raised in the most diverse ways. You could say that the entire community stepped forward once again. The regional area had Armenia in good memory. The Pentecostal congregation went at the forefront and company owners slashed prices or donated goods outright, the schools' students raised funds, Rotary joined in. Once again, it turned out that the Swedes are made of the right stuff when it comes to foreign and humanitarian aid!

Mrs. Charlene Pagett remembers the whole thing well. Charlene is the secretary of Caminul Felix's international board. After all, it was her husband, Bob, who once upon a time had invited the head of the Romanian Center for Disease Prevention to the U.S. and it was Bob who had been summoned to the meeting where Lars Hörnberg had been fired.

Charlene recounts:

"We had invited the children's choir to the U.S. and there were plans for a concert in Santa Cruz, California, in the Holy Cross Catholic Church. The acoustics in that church are amazing. The concert had been arranged on an ecumenical basis.

Attending the concert was a teacher from Scotts Valley. She had heard that we were sponsoring the choir's journey to the U.S., and one day, she came to our office and wanted to know a bit more about our organization, Assist International. She asked us about our project, and I told her of our plans to build a home for abandoned children. This lady is a Music teacher and she really liked our concert. When she was leaving the office, she said: 'Well, our family has a small trust. Why don't you send us a small application, because we might be interested in supporting your work in Romania?'

When she'd left our office, I told Bob about her visit. I said that we'll write a short description, because people like her don't like reading long harangues. So we wrote a couple of pages of an application. She came back and asked for a little more detailed description. Oh yes, we wrote and wrote. It took a few hours and then we sent the letter to her family trust. We thought that if we get 500 or 1,000 dollars, we should be happy.

A few weeks later, the whole family came into the office and it was exciting to listen to them. Well, they had decided to give 130,000 dollars to one of the homes in Romania! The reason was that the woman's grandmother had been Romanian and now, they wanted to do this in her memory.

We put together a construction team, and then we set off to build. Together with the different interest groups we had been in touch with during the course of the journey, the project was finished successfully. We call the house 'the Hancock House.'"

During one of my visits to Caminul Felix, I have come to know a wonderful "prankster" for a pastor and wind musician. That is Peter Jenkins from the Amblecote Christian Centre in England. He leads a large and growing mission congregation. He is an ace at playing the trombone and I have had the pleasure of playing together with him at some occasion. How did Peter Jenkins get into the picture with Caminul Felix?

"Well, a good friend of mine, John Wildrianne, called me one day and asked whether we could step in as hosts to a young student from their Bible college during the summer break," Peter recounts. "She was Romanian and couldn't finance her return trip home. Of course, she was welcome. Her name was Adriana Paul.

So, Adriana came, and the congregation took good care of her. We all liked Adriana very much. When she returned to Romania the following year, we visited her. We then met Linda and Lars Hörnberg at Caminul Felix where Adriana worked.

This was the beginning of an adventure both for me personally and my entire congregation. From the start, we had no idea where all this would lead us.

Later, I met John Wildrianne again. John had been a board member of Caminul Felix's international board for some time, and now I was asked to join the board – an incredible privilege! At the next board meeting, we had the shocking news that we perhaps would have to leave Caminul Felix 1 and that we probably had to start looking around for other homes for the children. Bob Pagett, our chairman, gave us the advice to build ten new houses that would become Caminul Felix 2 and to let the nations of the world be involved in the act. Aren't the Americans generous! So, before we had even started thinking about it, Bob took on the responsibility to let the Americans build seven of the houses! Then, he looked at me and asked: 'Well, what will the Brits do now?' What was I supposed to say? I said okay, my congregation will build one of the houses. At that moment, I didn't know how. I now had a difficult but self-assumed task to explain to my congregation why I'd taken the decision!

Yes, the congregation agreed to my proposal, and we raised about 17,000 pounds in the first offering. The congregation was with us! We'd understood the children's needs, and we saw our opportunities to help. Each and every one member of my congregation did their bit. We arranged auctions and we did all other kinds of possible and impossible things. Articles were written in the papers and the municipality stepped in."

"The house that the Brits built is called Lisa Potts' House, why is that, Peter?" I ask.

"Well, that's a good question. We were asked to name the house and we were thinking about putting our congregation's name on it. At that time, I was invited to a party with well-known people in society. Suddenly, I had an idea that I wrote down and brought to the party. At the dinner, a number of writers were going to present their new publications, and Lisa Pots would give a speech. She was one of the writers.

Lisa is well-known all over Great Britain, not least after a tragic event that happened at her hospital. She was working as a nurse in Wolverhampton when she was attacked by an insane man with a machete who caused her severe injuries. She was awarded the St. George Cross for heroically protecting the children who were in the vicinity of the attack. Lisa became the protecting symbol in person. Caring for the children. Letting your life constitute protection for the least among us.

I had of course already written her a letter to ask whether she wanted to come with me to Romania and be involved in what we were building. I headed off for the party. How I would be able to deliver the letter to her, I didn't know.

At the dinner, the chairman said that there would unfortunately not be any opportunity to ask Lisa any questions. But if anybody had a question, they could hand in a written one which she could late reply to. I had the letter in my pocket, so when others started writing down their questions on the paper napkins, I handed over my letter.

Later that evening, I went forward to Lisa, who wondered if it was I who wanted her to come to Romania. I replied affirmatively. She said that she had always wanted to travel to Romania but that she did not know anyone there. We decided on a date and we traveled to Caminul Felix and saw all that was happening. She got

Marcel Filip, Geo Dejeu and Paul Luncan with his wife.

involved in the work and in January, 2001, we had the dedication of our house!"

* * *

Monday, October 5, 2001, was a day of happiness, and our gratitude to the Lord was great. That was the day when Caminul Felix 2 was declared open.

Crowds had gathered for the dedication. Amongst them were the pioneers Linda and Lars Hörnberg with all of their staff, house parents and children who had already taken up residency in their houses.

Seeing all the nations' flags triumphantly flying in the wind around the large grassy court was a sight for sore eyes. It is like a cleverly doctored photo.

Familjen Simona and Emil Puscas outside Lisa Pott's house.

Peter Jenkins, Lisa Pott and John Wildrianne.

Over the widespread field, ten wonderful and spacious homes are towering. At the center, there is a green area which in turn is rounded off by a paved road. Every home has its own vegetable garden, its own special character since so many builders and individual donors have left their mark on the homes. A large number of trees have been planted in front of the houses so as to create some leafy green on the otherwise treeless field.

Here, the Romanian authority figures were now sitting in long lines, taking note of every element of the feast. Mayors and governors were here, the Swedish Embassy's people were here, Charlene and Bob Pagett, Peter Jenkins and John Wildrianne were here, and beside them, a large host of witnesses. But above all, the dedication was accompanied by resolve, personal faith and generous donation.

* * *

You already know that the Hörnberg's won the court verdict. Everything remained as it had been intended with Caminul Felix 1. Nothing had been taken away from the children. With the opening of Caminul Felix 2, the opportunities had become so much greater, greater than anybody else had been able to expect. There are now two family villages with a capacity for 250 children. The villages are now filled with children that are how large the need is. But there is still a world of unwanted and abandoned children in Oradea and around our world!

Chapter 18

The Academy

Through my connections inside and outside Romania, I have often heard that Caminul Felix stands for something completely new in the Romanian society. The concept for the abandoned and unwanted children's future that the Hörnberg's' vision has created is spreading in circuits that are important. The local head of the child custody board in Oradea, Ioan Groza, has copied the concept in almost all details. He says that Caminul Felix is of good example to the municipality. Therefore, there are now several small houses with a lesser number of children and staff in Oradea, which in many ways look like the concept that has been created at Caminul Felix. The large orphanages with hundreds of abandoned children are becoming fewer and fewer. Ioan Groza has even managed to produce temporary foster parents.

In conversations with the former county governor Petru Ungur, he emphasizes firmly the importance of the Caminul Felix spirit being spread throughout the country.

The principal Viorel Patre with his staff of teachers at the state school which 49 of the children from Caminul Felix attended emphasized very strongly the importance of the children getting the security that the family spirit creates.

Of course, the Caminul Felix doctor and psychiatrist Daniel Buzle agrees. Dr. Buzle has been at Caminul Felix ever since the start, and was, in addition, the director of the compound for a number of years.

The Hörnberg vision is alive and most definitely doing very well!

"Our vision and our concept are good enough for the whole world," Lars Hörnberg exclaims. He is proud and humble of his own and others' conclusion and the listener emotionally realizes that, that is how it is!

The Hörnberg vision cannot be limited. It is taking ground and it is becoming increasingly well-known in the circuits revolving around Caminul Felix in Romania and also in many other countries in the world.

* * *

Caminul Felix became the revolution of thought that was needed in the country. The attitude towards children who are unwanted, disabled or abandoned has changed fundamentally. At a visit that I did at the state-run treatment facility for neurological treatment of children in Oradea, I could not avoid noticing this, and I was very touched by it. I just had to ask if Adriana du Plessis at Casa Minunata had not exaggerated her description of the Romanians' previously negative attitudes towards such children. Because what I now saw was a warm and loving tenderness from the staff towards the children. After all, there couldn't have been such a change in only about ten years, could there? "Yes, absolutely," says Lars!

"There's a new attitude towards the children!"

One of the people from Caminul Felix who has meant incredibly much for changing the attitudes at the mentioned state-run treatment facility is Adi Bulc. He was one of the first house parents at Caminul Felix 1. Adi used to be a professional soccer player and has been a coach for youngsters in a number of sports inside and outside Caminul Felix throughout the years. He could not refrain from helping out when he saw the shortcomings at the treatment facility. It was not quite his business. But when he saw, for example, the need of an elevator between the floors, he had an elevator installed, and a Rotary club in the U.S. paid for it. Before that, the children and youngsters had been carried between the floors. Or when the pools with warm and mineral-rich volcanic water used for treatment needed repair, well, and then Adi did that too.

There is much else that needs to be done at the treatment facility. When we toured it with Adi Bulc for "inspection," he suddenly noticed that one of the handrails in one of the pools had rusted to pieces and needed to be replaced in order to avoid cutting injuries. Lars immediately took out his cell phone and called the builder Radu Cun who straight away came over to take measurements and make new handrails from stainless steel. Radu Cun is well-known to many Swedish builders. He is the builder who was responsible for the work when Caminul Felix 1 was erected.

Romania used to be the major example of how scores of abandoned children had been neglected. For example, who does not remember the so-called "sewer children" whom the state knew about, but whom it did not do anything about. Or the "crib kids" at the institutions. Romania was really known for this all over the world. But with the Caminul Felix concept and the new family spirit that exists there, Romania now has a chance instead to become the country that shows the best way to a good society, where the children come first.

* * *

Caminul Felix is the embryo for a worldwide social revival to save the world's abandoned children.

For a few years, Lars Hörnberg has spoken about his vision to create education opportunities for social educationalists from all over Europe. What social workers from other countries have seen at Caminul Felix is something they want to copy. One highly tropical country right now is Thailand. The place for education in Oradea that Lars Hörnberg is talking about is an Academy, and that would become a gift for the children of the world.

"Unless we get an Academy, Caminul Felix will only remain an island both in time and space and will only remain for as long as there are enthusiasts," Lars says.

The new concept that Caminul Felix has introduced in

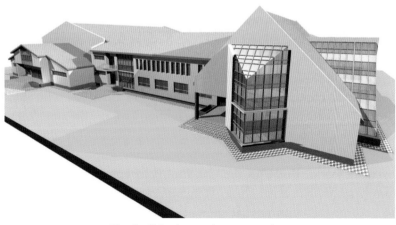

Sketch of the dream about an academy.

Romania and for the needs of other countries could mean that the relation between new parents and children will become a stronger unifying bond than the blood-relationship is between biological parents and children.

Lars takes the Bible to help him support his opinion. God decided to take mankind to heart. "He birthed us again through his promise," he quotes. "He asked a carpenter to become the adoptive father of his son," Lars continues, "and Joseph gave the world an image of what a real father-son relation could be like. God gave the world's most important job to the simplest people, to Mary and Joseph, who had no previous experience of being parents. And, of course, no other new parents have any experience of that either. The world's most important task is to be a parent, and nobody has that experience from the beginning," Lars says.

* * *

Talking about the Academy project to be: Marcel Filip, Bob Pagett, Senator Radu Tirle, Adriana du Plessis, John Wildrianne, Governor Ilie Boljan, Jaco du Plessis.

The relation with Oradea's mayor is very good. It is so good that the mayor is happy to see that the Academy will be built together with the municipality. Then, the building permit, which will attract a cost of about SEK 1 million, could be paid by the municipality.

The Academy will be built in three sections. The first section will consist of a college at a total of twelve classrooms and a library, specialized at the exclusive knowledge that our world needs to save the abandoned children. The other section will be a sports center with a professional stage and kitchen and be convertible for weddings, concerts and feasts. The third section will contain offices for Caminul Felix and for all the units and the sister organizations that have sprouted together with Caminul Felix.

* * *

We put forward our opinions in conversations with the Swedish Embassy in Bucharest. The Ambassador couple Lotta and Svante Kilander treated us to a fine dinner. Together with their staff, David Lunderquist and Börje Duvell, they received us cordially and friendly when we visited them in Bucharest. The hope is that the Academy could and should be funded by the EU. The fact is that so far, no state or international funds have been used in the gigantic project called Caminul Felix. It has consistently been single individuals' gifts and initiatives that have characterized the work. Now, it should be time for all of Europe to get such an Academy. That is Caminul Felix's offer to Europe!

"But unless we get an Academy, Caminul Felix will only remain an island both in time and space and will only remain for as long as there are enthusiasts," Lars Hörnberg did say.

Some house parents have fostered an entire rising generation and have other tasks within Caminul Felix. Eli and Marcel are on the management of the Foundation. Lidia and Mircea follow Caminul Felix's ideas of additional fields, and perhaps their next area of responsibility will be in an African country. Who knows! Simona and Geo Dejeu have also moved on and returned to their professional roles in society. (Pictured: Marcel Filip, Bob Pagett, Senator Radu Tirle, Adriana du Plessis, John Wildrianne, County Governor Ilie Boljan, Jaco du Plessis)

Chapter
19

All these volunter workers

Lasse was constantly soaking with sweat and changed his work clothes twice a day!

The work needed to be done. Resting was something that you could do when you were back at home in Sweden!

Lasse, with the surname Carlsson, wanted to give his contribution to the children. The effort meant puttying and painting walls, windows and façades. Neither he nor the other men considered themselves to be professionals, but the master house-painter Eric Svensson was responsible for the team from Vetlanda. Eric supervised his workers and Lasse was promoted to deputy master!

Eric Lundahl was responsible for the compound's locking systems, which meant that one main key would fit all doors. But Eric found himself in trouble when he discovered that that had been an attractive item. The boxes had been ripped open and both locks and keys were missing. How he solved that is another untold story, but I wonder if he did not get a few extra grey hairs in the process.

The mission for the team from Vetlanda was to paint, lay pipes or cut carpets, to tile and to do carpentry work. The seven houses had already been erected, that was something that other teams had done previously, and it had happened fast. Team Boro had supplied the houses and the happy, bright colors were in place when the team from Vetlanda arrived with Bengt Arvidsson at the wheel.

It was Bengt Olzon who had the idea for an effort. Bengt was a merchant and had made sure during all of his life that the city's ladies in Vetlanda were well-dressed. Qvinny was the name of the boutique in Stationsgatan, and there, his wife Anne Marie was the boss, while Bengt ran the office and the finances. When Bengt had a major birthday, he invited his friends to a large feast at the local recreation park and raised money for Erikshjälpen.

Photo: Bengt Olzon

Bengt and Erikshjälpen used to collaborate. The collaboration consisted, amongst other things, of Bengt and his wife being sponsors, and the foundation sending money to Bengt's and his wife's sponsored children in Romania.

It did not take long before Bengt got in touch with Göran Ivarsson at Erikshjälpen and inquired whether the Hörnberg's in

Bengt Arvidsson. Nice with a break!

Oradea needed any manpower. Oh yes!

Bengt raised the issue with some of his Rotary friends and that is how things happened. A team was arranged quickly, and a minivan was borrowed from the car salesman Gert Nyström and the trip went long through Europe to Oradea.

To the six gentlemen, Romania was a new experience, of course. It was like driving back to the Sweden of their childhood. In the countryside, horses with buggies roamed the roads. In the villages, there were long rows of women selling beautifully embroidered tablecloths and needlework. Others sold sausages or sunflower seeds. Bengt "Pomona" Johansson, who had sold thousands of kilos of sunflower seeds at home in Vetlanda in his shop in Lasarettsgatan, could hardly believe his eyes when he saw how the ladies sold a handful of seeds for some petty change just to survive the day. "Pomona" ordered the driver to stop the van so that he could buy some seeds. He took out his pocketbook and gave

Photo: Bernt Einarsson

From the Romanian countryside.

the largest bill he had to the lady with the seeds. "It was like she had won a million crowns when she saw the money," said Bengt "Pomona".

They probably did take one day or another off, I understand. Of course, there was much to see. For example the dripstone caves or Timisoara, where the revolution once started. At one occasion, they went to the Hungarian border, where there was a decent fish restaurant. The food came on plates after you had selected your own grass carp in the aquarium. They were beefy fish taking all the space on the plates, it tasted well but there was nothing else served with it. Yes, it was tasty, unless they had fried the fish in rancid butter, but so what? It was good enough anyway! In order to get to the restaurant that was situated so close to the Hungarian border, they were forced to hand in their passports to the police who guarded the area.

One Sunday, there was a real party. They travelled out in the

The paint gang from Vetlanda.

countryside together with a guide. Upon arrival at the restaurant, which was the destination for their journey, they ordered a three-course meal. It tasted excellent and when the check came, they could not believe their eyes. The price was 130 SEK for eight and a half people, the half person was the guide's lad! And then, you also had a cup of coffee included!

Gas was a whole different chapter, of course. There was a shortage of gas, and the lines to the gas stations were several kilometers long.

"I did think it was a bit unfair," said Bengt, in a Swedish manner. "The foreign cars were given priority, while the taxis used up what little gas they had in the line up to the gas station!"

The team from Vetlanda travelled down to Oradea twice that year, 1991. When they were finished, they gathered together their painters' clothes and laid them in a barrel to be burned. The next morning, it was time to go home, and then the barrel was empty. The clothes had been attractive items. You couldn't just burn them! When they had gone for a bit into Hungary, one of the men said: "I could have left all my other clothes as well. It would have been enough to take me home with the clothes I have on me!"

But they couldn't turn back. They had gone too far, and moreover, it was not all that simple to make it back through the customs office.

"We'll never forget that we had the chance to make an effort for the abandoned and unwanted children in Romania," says Eric Svensson. "How many new friends we made, how friendly the Romanians are. Being able to work together with Radu and Victor was fun. The Hörnberg's were also easy to deal with!"

The Vetlanda team's effort amounted to 350 work hours. In Sweden, the corresponding work effort would have cost about

SEK 75,000. Many square meters were painted. You understand that when the total floor space for the seven houses is about 2,300 square meters.

* * *

Now, it seems as though there were only old men from Sweden investing time and energy to make Caminul Felix come true. There were of course a number of ladies among all the men. Of course, they did more or less what needed to be done. Well, the hard labor was spared them. But Kerstin Fälth and her women friends did not shy away from anything, actually. They donned the painters' clothes, they hung curtains and "architected" the

Romanian road builder.

laundry room. Linda Hörnberg knew what she wanted and left her distinctive mark on the General Activities House. There, long tables were laid for the workers, and there, the room for a doctor's surgery and a music room for growing musicians were furnished.

* * *

Småland and Västergötland produced most of the workers' teams, but some came all the way from Dalarna. It is impossible to mention everybody by name. In Värnamo, Caminul Felix was rooted for all future, or so it seems. Stig Björhag – the master house-painter – will not let go of Caminul Felix. He travels there about once a year, and the minivan is packed with enthusiasts who controlled the standards of the houses at Caminul Felix. If the houses need a makeover, it gets done. Bright colors should shine from the houses, the locks should work and the washing machines should spin. The stove should heat and the ventilation should work. That is what Stig Björhag and his colleagues makes sure happens!

All these blessed volunteer workers!

Chapter 20

'It's only grace,' said Henry Nyman

He looks at me, Henry Nyman, when I ask the question and he asks to get to about the matter for a while. The rest of us go on talking for half an hour or so, and there are many memories that turn up. We laugh heartily and Rolf Sjöö tells us about something that makes his voice shiver and tears well up in his eyes. He remembers the children whom he was able to help provide a home they had never had. There are so many precious images that surface from his sub consciousness when Caminul Felix comes up.

"GRAAACE!" Henry interjects when he has finished thinking. "Write that it's only GRACE from the beginning to the end! Imagine that we got to be part of this! I carry great gratitude with me through life. Imagine that God gave me this experience!"

That was the response to my question how he would like to summarize the intense time during which Caminul Felix was built.

We are sitting at home in my house talking. The hours fly. My wife Gudrun has, during all these years, "lived" with the first children in the first house. She mentions the parents by name and actually the first children too. She felt like an overjoyed midwife who day after day handed over new children to longing parents. Then, the other five houses were filled with happy children and their new parents. Gudru[1] n also decided the happy colors of the houses in the family village together with Uncle Erik'swidow, Ulla Nilsson.

At the other side of the coffee table, Henry and Rolf, the portal figures in the Boro team, are thus seated. Henry, with an incredibly strong network of suppliers which he has built during his time as a sales manager at Team Boro. Henry is a string personality with a great faith in God mixed with a large portion of humor. It was not only the delivery of prefab house blocks, because that was something he had close at hand. Much and many things were also needed: white goods, windows, locks, carpets, electrical appliances, stoves and so on in order for the work at the family village to move on and be completed as smoothly as possible. The construction teams could, of course, only stay for a few weeks at a time, and it was important that the work was not obstructed by delayed goods. Henry picked up the phone, and everyone he contacted could contribute goods, sometimes for free, sometimes at heavily reduced prices. Today, Henry still remains full of admiration over how Göran Ivarsson at Erikshjälpen could produce transports at incredibly low costs.

There sat Rolf, the construction leader, who with his "sharp" modern Swedish tools introduced a completely new way to

Rolf Sjöö and Henry Nyman

---

1   "Uncle Erik", Erik Nilsson (1929-1966) was the founder of Erikshjälpen, ERIKS Development Partner. –Translator's Note

handle raw materials, and who set about leading the work. During the Communist era, work leadership was in the style of giving orders, but Rolf introduced "confidence and own responsibility" for the workers. They showed plenty of skill and radiated with true working joy. They had a value as God's collaborators in that way.

Rolf speaks in construction terms such as "capillary-breaking foundation materials" and "insulated slab edge elements". He talks about millimeters and macadam, steel girders and excavators from the 1940s. He remembers Radu, a young Romanian receptive construction engineer, who had never been outside the borders of his homeland but who sucked in Rolf's knowledge. With such a collaborator, Rolf could easily teach the Swedish construction technology to the Romanian construction workers. One of Radu's assistants, the measuring engineer Gabriel, quickly learned how to handle the leveling-instrument, which is an ultramodern laser with a sound indicator.

But, of course, sometimes Rolf needed to lend a few extra hands. Not concerning his workers, because he only had a nice and fun time with them, but concerning local authorities and suppliers. As, for example, when the foundation slabs were to be cast for the houses. The insulated slab edge elements were in place, as was the capillary-breaking foundation material, and then the concrete trucks were supposed to come. The slab was to be cast. Then, one single truck came, and no more. Rolf had ordered ten trucks for each slab. Every one of my readers of course understands that it was important that the entire concrete slab was "cured" at once. Now, only one truck came.

Rolf probably gets a bit aggravated and throws himself into Radu's car and drives over to the concrete supplier, who at first does not understand why Rolf needs to have ten trucks available and ready for each day's need. There wasn't that much of a hurry, was there? Rolf's Romanian is, at the beginning of his stay in the country, not all that fluent, and Radu's English is probably of the same quality. Rolf grabs a sheet of paper and draws ten concrete trucks in a long row and writes "60 minutes" between each drawn truck. A smile starts playing in the corner of the concrete guy's mouth. He glances up and nods his head understandingly. The next day, the ten concrete trucks arrive one hour apart, one by one until all the seven slabs have been cast! From the third concrete slab on, the Romanians handled the foundation work by themselves. The laser shone along with the Romanians, and the indicator was beeping. They did a good job with the new construction technology that they had learned.

Such intense traffic was something the poor concrete trucks had not experienced for years and years. No wonder one of them caught fire and just died in the flames! No people were hurt, luckily enough, but it sure did look very dramatic when thick, black smoke was belching out from the area where Life's Own University was being built!

Truck on fire.

Or when Rolf thought that the caterpillar was moving at a snail's pace up and down the pits where the slabs were to be cast. He leaped up to the driver and pointed at the lever which read "idling," and with a convincing gesture, he argued that it was supposed to be pushed to the bottom. It's supposed to be full speed! Yes, of course, the only problem was that when the caterpillar absorbed the acceleration force, the driving belt went all south or the wheel-loader which did not have any brakes! But that was solved by one man being on standby with a plank which he threw in front of the wheels when his colleague up in the bucket yelled "stop".

Rolf's and Radu's Romanian builders were present during the entire construction phase. They have learned a fine craft. Working with bottom insulation, erecting the wall blocks, placing roof trusses and installing ventilation shafts. Rolf explained the necessity for the houses to be ventilated. Every average family exhales three buckets of water per day, which needs to be sucked out of the

Excavator model 40's.

houses to prevent them from becoming moldy and sick. If the family then consists of 20 people, it is more than necessary to have proper ventilation. This was something Henry had also thought of. Apart from the new exhaust air systems, he had gotten double-glazed windows, and they could be opened. Perhaps a window pane could sometimes be smashed. It is, after all, something that little boys tend to do from time to time –then, you need to be able to replace the panes without it taking too much effort.

During the year of 1991, six family homes were built, and a large multi-purpose house at Caminul Felix. The total floor area was 2,300 square meters. The cost in cash was about SEK 6 million. That means less than half the price of what it would normally supposed to have cost. The head of Boro, Curt Wrigfors, had given Henry and Rolf a carte blanche to procure the materials, and given them work hours at their own disposal, and the suppliers were generous. Everyone wanted to join in. Everything became so much cheaper that it cannot even be mentioned. That is what it was like with all the goods that were transported over from Sweden.

The construction teams had things approved for them. Their salary was paid by unemployment benefits and trade unions. The employment offices in Sweden had approved that laid off construction workers could make an effort abroad.

The fact that Sweden one year later experienced its most difficult downturn since the last world war was of course not because of Caminul Felix being built so cheaply and because the suppliers join in in full numbers, as Henry says, "We made the effort at precisely the right moment! One year later, it wouldn't have been possible!"

* * *

Rolf Sjöö often visits different churches and other contexts and talks about the exciting Caminul Felix times. He captivates his audience and the audience is moved to tears when he tells them about the best time of his life. That was when he saw the children coming from the sewers or their cardboard boxes for houses and moved into the children's villages, where friendly parents took care of them, gave them food, beds, a sense of home, and love and made sure that they were given medical care and the chance to go to school.

Perhaps Rolf is telling this to the audience which perhaps once upon a time gave money in the collection for a spade or a washing-basin, how that money has changed the standards of a entire country and given the country a completely new view of its children. How their offerings for a stove or for a washing-machine became the foundation for a new life for young people building up their Romania or travelling to Moldova to give their people the Gospel. Eventually, Rolf's audience connects the dots into that if the outer man becomes clean, you also want your inner man to become clean – or if he means it the other way round the truth is both one thing and another, and both Rolf and the audience are powerfully moved by the message.

Chapter

21

Thailand

When we had just opened the first family village Caminul Felix in Oradea and everyone was euphoric over the jewel that the family village constituted in the Romanian society and how the result of donors' love was standing there as a prototype for the optimal foreign aid, well, then the Romanian TV asked the question to Erikshjälpen's chairman P-O Klint whether this was not only the beginning of a chain of similar family villages around Romania. I heard P-O Klint reply that it was an attractive thought, and that Erikshjälpen perhaps could take that to heart as a continued challenge. I remember how I was almost terrified trying to fend off the thought. After all, I knew what it had cost in terms of money, and not least in terms of work efforts and transportation.

It soon turned out that the Romanian authorities themselves opened up to the idea of family villages. The local child custody board's head in Oradea, Ioan Groza, has in almost every detail copied the family concept that Caminul Felix introduced. The former County Governor, Petru Ungur, emphasizes firmly the importance of the Caminul Felix spirit being spread throughout the country. And then, I did, of course mention earlier on in this book how the Ministry of Education wanted to help write the curriculum for the special needs schools in the country.

It did not take long until also neighboring countries including Moldova and Ukraine heard about what was being built in Romania, and conveyed their wishes for similar investments in a Caminul Felix spirit in their own countries. Indeed, such requests came in all the way from Africa.

The vision that the Hörnberg's birthed and let grow has now matured in order to be reproduced, but has the founder and the caretaker of the Caminul Felix concept, Lars Hörnberg, the time and the energy to listen to other countries' needs to save their abandoned children?

Well, those of us who listen to Lars when he excites his audience understand that his absolute calling is to spread the vision further. I do not know of anybody else who is so enthusiastically on fire for such a spread than Lars himself. His vision is not being limited by national borders. Often, you hear him speak about the many millions of lonely orphans in the world. His closest aides are standing loyally by his side. What has happened in Romania with Caminul Felix is, so far, unique in the foreign aid community and the world needs to know about it.

So, I will let him recount the next phase of the development of Caminul Felix, but this time, in Thailand, himself:

"It isn't easy work to have an idea in your head. It becomes even harder when the idea's in your heart. Then, it becomes the master of all other plans, and convinces you that it can be realized – even if nothing in your head speaks in favor of it. Going against your heart's conviction expresses indifference to life's true purpose and force. It's wise to search the channels that give us the possibility to support life.

Caminul Felix's family activities have so powerfully proven superior to all other care for abandoned children, that is, the idea that gives a child a loving pair of parents and all the resources that life requires.

Those who have seen the power in this way of working know that it is time to stop building institutions for children, the classic orphanages with large halls and impersonal relations with staff. That sort of care often isn't any developing care, only storage. It was considered cheap, but it has turned out to be the cheapest we've done for our children there was nothing of value that was given to their lives through it. It's true that a bed is always better than the sidewalk, and a meal is better than starving. It's also true that the millions of children who don't have a secure family will always miss the role model of how to build their lives, the one that is hereditary in our senses, the one that was given by the great Father's heart. That is why the many children of our time need to be given a family.

Somebody told me: 'Lars, we in the West are the richest generation ever. Basically all of us have more than we need and we'll die with unused bank accounts. Our children have money, they don't need ours. Tell us what to do to take proper care of our resources and make a difference. Tell us in plain language what we can accomplish. Let the big opportunities come, the ones with a purpose and competence for our lives. Offer us commitment. Challenge us!'"

* * *

Intermission

The world's abandoned children do not only exist in Romania. We had heard Lars say that many times. Now, the doors were opened to Thailand, and things hit the ground running from the start. Of course, there were obstacles to overcome. Many meetings and one setback or another took place, and much text was written in minutes and our friends at the administration in Aneby had a lot to do.

Let's take it from the beginning! I do think I play a certain role in the process myself, even though it is of a different kind then the people's tasks you have already met in this book. The thing is, I was given the task to try to write down the story of the leap from Romania to Thailand.

The following chapters are partly of a different character. The 20 first chapters in this book are about Romania and want to

Bonds of friendship between Thailand and Sweden.

reflect the prelude to a continuation that we have not yet seen the end of. The next three chapters of what will now follow recounts some people's influence on the Thailand project. People whom you have not met earlier. It is about their background way back in time and what impact their experiences in their early young lives are having today when Felix Family Village in Thailand is now being built.

Perhaps you feel that the following chapters could have become a book of its own. Perhaps you are right, but now, you get these chapters too included in the deal, so to speak!

So come with us into a new phase of visions to give abandoned children a mother and a father!

Chapter 22

Siam

After almost 70 years, I still remember the war in Siam, as Thailand was called in those days. What captured the attention of a five-year-old was the strange and exciting black and white images in the newspaper; soldiers wading through marshes with their weapons lifted above their heads, horses who ploughed through water and cross-country jeeps forcing their way across rivers without any difficulties. In my world, cars were such vehicles that were driving around on Jönköpingsvägen in Värnamo. I had hardly seen any soldiers in real life, with the exception of the military convoy which one day hummed up the main street in our town. My mother and I were standing outside the Röda Kvarn Cinema waiting for the convoy to come. The reason why we knew that the military convoy would come that way and on that day was probably because my father had written us a letter from somewhere in Sweden where he was on emergency military service, as it was called. Perhaps any of my readers remembers the gray and blue envelopes which the armed forces' staff used and which included a stamped reply envelope with a pre-printed address code that would reach the conscript husband wherever he was in the country.

So we were standing outside Röda Kvarn Cinema, as my mother and father had agreed. When the convoy drove through town, my father would try to make himself visible right there and then. That also happened. He sat on the flatbed of a truck among many other soldiers. They had folded up the gray truck cover and right there at Röda Kvarn, I saw my first soldier. It was my father waving and whooping together with the other soldiers on the flatbed. Later, when the war had ended, he would recount the occasion when he as a 30-year-old family father had seen his little family standing there on the sidewalk waving at him. Many other family fathers on the flatbed had also discovered their loved ones. When the convoy disappeared up Highway No. 1, there was a sense of unease among the men on the truck flatbed and the silence became deafening with longing for home and family. For a moment, so close, but yet so far away.

Where was the convoy going? Nobody knew. "A Swede Keeps Silent" was a slogan that could be read on billboards and in newspapers.

When my father after a year or so was back home, he used to tell us the exciting military stories from his time in the emergency military service. How he, as a runner, rode a bolting horse through central Malmö without a chance of stopping the horse until the frightening cars started becoming more scarce at the edge of town. How he saw the anti-aircraft defense shooting down a German airplane that had strayed in over Skåne, and later, how an English Flying Fortress in the Luleå area had been forced to make an emergency landing. How frozen he had been in the tents with wooden fires in the snowy and cold Lapland and how he struggled to keep the horses alive, how he watered the platoon's horses and found hay and concentrated feed for his four-legged friends. How many times after the end of the war that I asked him to tell me these hair-raising military stories there on the edge of my bed in the apartment that we rented from the Gustavssons in Kvarnängsgatan, I can only guess. My mother had then gone to singing practice in the Bethel chapel or was knitting completely necessary winter clothes together with the sewing bee ladies.

Anyway, I studied the images from Siam carefully, and perhaps I fantasized that one of the soldiers wading through the river was my own father. The fact that it was the French or the Japanese who had invaded Siam or the Thai who were defending their own land was of course nothing I comprehended. The images now come to me as sure as fate whenever I visit Thailand. I see them now as I am writing these words in a hotel room in Chiang Rai in northern Thailand. Siam, so mythical and beautiful and which was struck by war machines of madness. Gruesome, but, to a five-year-old, a fascinating air of war.

Thailand became a tangible reality to me when I came to Erikshjälpen in 1980, as Erikshjälpen then had a lot of connections in Thailand. There were orphanages and social projects financed by Erikshjälpen. In the South, the missionaries Eva and Dan Olofsson had a ministry to the lepers, perhaps one of the very first leprosy projects at all which were supported by a Swedish aid organization. Some 15 years later, Eva Olofsson would surprise the Scandinavian audience with a new unique project which was named Baan Chivit Mai. The project found its beginnings in Bangkok's slums and later as a village in Chiang Rai where girls who risked being sold into prostitution were saved to a decent life. After a few years, Eva opened yet another home for children infected with HIV and who risked developing AIDS.

Eva Olofsson has an outstanding capacity for making connections across all borders. Through the Swedish Embassy in Bangkok, such a contact emerged with the Swedish Royal Court. I and my wife were invited by Eva to dinner at the Grand Hotel in Stockholm with the Swedish King and Queen and many other guests, including the vocal group Triple & Touch. There, Queen Silvia handed over a check worth SEK 350,000 to Eva Olofsson for her work among the children of the slums. A few years later, the Swedish King and Queen visited the children's village in Chiang Rai and were able to hear the stories and the testimonies first-hand about what God is able to do.

To us at Erikshjälpen, Thailand became the base for various aid projects in the neighboring countries of Cambodia, Burma and Laos, but above all in Vietnam and Bangladesh. Eva Olofsson's husband Dan was able to build more than 3,000 houses for refugees from regions around Hanoi, who had fled south to the Saigon area, before Saigon fell into the Communists' hands. Later, some refugees would come from the infamous massacre of the village of Song My. The village had been mowed down by American soldiers and they had neither spared women nor children. Those who managed to escape took the name of their village, Song My, with them and gave the new village that name.

What an experience to get the chance to look up one of those villages at the end of the 1990s. We came just in time for the congregation's service one Sunday morning and took part in it. What Dan Olofsson had planted had survived all the horrors of war and a crowd of believers regularly gathered together for church.

I visited Cambodia in the early 1990s. The contacts with the persecuted Christians in the capital Phnom Penh were taken through YWAM, a youth organization which had its office in Bangkok. In mysterious ways, we ended up in a secret prayer meeting in Phnom Penh after having changed cars a few times to shake off the secret police that were following us. A few years later, we were free to work socially in Cambodia.

It is also at this time that connections were established in Burma, and a well-known and respected pastor, Myo Chit, could open many doors for the type of evangelical/social work that Erikshjälpen represented.

One day, I was invited to a cocktail party at the Ethiopian ambassador's in Stockholm. I had been to similar events earlier, and the social mingling always used to be of some benefit to me as head of Erikshjälpen.

This time, I noticed that the Ethiopian ambassador is standing talking to the ambassador from Laos. They are looking my way knowingly and soon I am involved in a conversation with the ambassador from Laos who asks me to visit him sometime at the embassy on the Stora Essingen island in Stockholm. I visited him on several occasions. The visits to the embassy eventually resulted in a trip to Laos together with him.

In the Laotian capital Vientiane, we had meetings with government members who gave Erikshjälpen the status to start huge projects in the Communist country. Since then, Erikshjälpen has had several aid workers in the country, and at the very moment I am writing these words at the hotel in Chiang Rai, I have met Madeleine and Inge Ekelyck from Huskvarna who used to work in Laos but who are now responsible for Baan Chivit Mai. We have just completed the 20th anniversary of Baan Chivit Mai's establishment in the country.

So you have understood that Thailand became an important point of connection to me, and a center for Erikshjälpen in Asia. It goes without saying that I had not a clue that my life would take such a large part of the country I had been fascinated by as a five-year-old with the wading soldiers in Siam's rivers.

Water would be at the center of events much later. It would revolve around the tsunami that washed away Phuket and large parts of the tourist centers.

Chapter 23

The guys of Filadelfia

In order to understand the connection between the Felix family villages in Romania and Thailand and prayer meetings in the Filadelfia Church in Stockholm in the 1950s, it could be interesting to look into a few guys' commitment to prayer, Bible reading and evangelism in those days.

This chapter is about the foundation that Lars Hörnberg had, backed by eight guys which included Jarl Josefsson and Börje Kindström.

Pastor Bo Hörnberg was a collaborator of Lewi Pethrus together with Martin Tornell. A legendary leadership within the Pentecostal movement is the right word. The Sunday evening revival meetings gathered many participants, including children and youth. Bo Hörnberg, commonly dubbed Bosse, went "fishing" among the pews and helped many young people forward to the mercy seat where your soul would be saved. Bosse's own boys, Lars and Bengt, were probably saved in the process, so to speak, their Dad was after all a pastor, and as a family father, Bosse had planted a consciousness early in Lars about leadership in God's congregations, which he later on developed successfully as a teenager and an adult.

Many years ago, I heard the stories about these guys' prayer meetings in the Filadelfia Church in Stockholm. Down below the large church at Rörstrandsgatan was the so-called 500 Room, where the young people gathered for prayer after the Sunday evening services, mostly very loud prayer. There were prophetical messages and there, you were thoroughly baptized in the Holy Spirit. Life-changing decisions were taken there, and many people who are well-known in the movement today have their deep roots in the spiritual soil that was cultivated in the 500 Room.

One of the guys in the gang was called Jarl Josefsson. He had initially mumbled something inaudible as Bosse during his "fishing" had asked if Jarl was saved, so the decision tarried for a while. Jarl was one of six siblings who grew up in Stadshagen on the Kungsholmen island. Their mother and father were deeply involved in the Filadelfia Church. Their father played the double bass in the string orchestra and the bass tuba in the brass band and sang bass in the men's choir. No wonder that Jarl later in life became instrumental in one company after another.

The parents struggled hard with their economy. His mother worked as a shop assistant, washed up in the delicatessen department after the day's sales, mopped the floor and cleaned up. Jarl's father was a house-painter by profession, but was usually laid off during the winter due to lack of work. He then looked for work within snow-clearance or in the free port. But it was Filadelfia's activities that occupied him in his spare time. Both parents sang in the choir with Karl-Erik Svedlund as their director. Jarl's mother made sure that the little home was always open to anyone who just wanted to pop in for a visit, and many, many people got to know the home which was located in the huge large-family house in Stadshagen on the island of Kungsholmen. During the so called Preachers' Week in December, a few pastors from the countryside stayed in the Josefssons' crammed spaces. The family squeezed into a couple of the three rooms and the "country brothers" got the best beds. That home actually had one of the very first TV sets in the country. The brother Bernt had been given the chance to work with people who brought the TV development in the country forward. Perhaps the very largest part of the Filadelfia congregation's members watched TV in the Josefsson home for the first time. TV was, in those days, something which was supposed to be watched in total darkness, and when the lights went on after broadcast hours had ended, you also saw pastors and elders loitering along the walls.

As mentioned, the family consisted of six children, parents, and sometimes guests or relatives who would spend the night in the little apartment. One toilet was available to this multitude of people which was crowding at the Josefsson home!

"In such an atmosphere, nobody can survive as a non-believer," said Jarl.

Happy children in the Felix Village in Thailand.

It goes without saying that all the Josefsson children were saved and still are.

"Our home was characterized by a high degree of spirituality," he continues.

Perhaps most of the youngsters in the 500 Room came from similar domestic conditions, but the experiences in the 500 Room and the importance of the fostering of their homes was nothing you could fend off. You hold your experiences from your youth in high esteem. They are a safe base for life, and the memories are dearly treasured.

Jarl and I are sitting at the river in Bangkok at the end of 2009. The taxi boats are darting back and forth on the mighty river while we try to sing from our memories the songs that were being used when we grew up. We have been visiting the Felix family village in Surat Thani in southern Thailand. We have seen what salvation at an early age and a purposeful life has resulted in. With 50 years of perspective back in time, you understand today what an incredible blessing it was to have a clear purpose with your life and your forthcoming service in God's kingdom already as a teenager. Jarl recounts his upbringing and his life, his radical salvation experience around the age of 12, his baptism in deep water and soon after baptism in the Holy Spirit with mighty glossolalia as a sign of being filled with the Spirit. Jarl had cultivated a desire that his baptism in the Holy Spirit would become a clear-cut baptism in the Holy Spirit, without anybody helping him "through," as it was sometimes called.

One evening, Jarl makes his way to a solitary place in one corner of the 500 Room. Jarl is overwhelmed by God's presence. God's Spirit touches his inner being, and it does not take long until he speaks in tongues, beautifully but loudly. He is so mightily overwhelmed by his baptism in the Holy Spirit that everyone in the room lift their heads in surprise from their kneeling positions at the pews. Where is he, Jarl, we hear his powerful voice but we don't see him!

As we sit by the river in Bangkok, talking and humming the old tunes, we are both moved to tears by how the times and living conditions have changed, but we have kept our faith in God's faithful guidance throughout the years. What grace to having been molded by believing parents! What a benefit to have been coached by wise congregation pastors during the transitional teenage times.

It was thus a wonderful band of brothers which was always present at the prayer meetings in the 500 Room after the revival meetings on Sunday evenings. They were between 15 and 17 years old. In the prayer meetings, there was also supposed to be singing and playing, if necessary. The young people of Filadelfia had ample opportunities to pursue their music. Jarl played in the brass band conducted by Birger Burman. Lars Hörnberg and Einar Bothén could play the guitar, and Jarl's twin brother Järt soon got started on his father's double bass. Lennart Lindström played the piano, Gunnar Carstelius and Hasse Wahlberg also joined in from the beginning.

They formed NSP, Nio Stockholms-Pojkar (Nine Stockholm Boys). Of course, NSP was a beginning protest movement against the traditional musical style in church. There, there was always singing from the hymnal Segertoner, and the string band sounded its own special way. Karl-Erik Svedlund's choral style had not yet become popular among the young people. The boys felt that Svedlund and other traditional director's complicated things.

Nine boys thus formed NSP and traveled the length and breadth of the country with a small songbook with red plastic covers. Lennart Lindström, with his fantastic piano playing, was quite a rock, and there was rhythm in Järt's double bass. Lars

Hörnberg played the guitar together with Einar Bothén.

"His name is Jesus, He's still alive, He is the same one for every time. He cures the sick and restores the ill. Yes, everything is laid under Him."

The song sounded mightily during visits to Sundsvall and Ystad when they did not sing at home in their own congregation. Because they were often on tour.

On one occasion, the NSP were invited to the prison in Ystad. The song "His name is Jesus…" touched the inmates deeply. Börje boldly testified about delivery from sin in Jesus' name.

"Come to our tent meetings in the park," Börje cried out to the inmates.

"Yes, if only we could," one prisoner answered. "But we're locked up! If you can help us out of here we'll be happy to come," the inmate pleaded.

The NSP and an ecumenically-based brass band were even called to a tent campaign in Beirut, Lebanon, where Dr. Samuel Doctorian had a flourishing evangelical ministry.

Bo Hörnberg went with the boys on tour preaching and coaching them, as it is called nowadays. But the preaching was soon taken over by Lars Hörnberg, and Bosse stayed at home.

Lars was a grave preacher. He studied the Bible and he expanded on the texts and he argued that God held the answer to all of life's questions. Just like his father, he went down among the church pews after the sermon, "fishing" and pleading with both old and young for them to let themselves be saved.

The prayer meetings continued, the Bible reading increased, and to Lars, Jarl and Börje, the search for the Bible's answers in crucial life decisions was of great and decisive importance. Börje Kindström was exceptionally true to Scripture. You could tell that from his worn-out and well-read Bible.

During their late teens, the three guys had serious discussions about Biblical issues and teenage theology, amongst other things, they held lively discussions about the choice of a spouse. How were you supposed to find the right person? They turned through the Bible pages and they carefully scrutinized the texts in the Old and the New Testament to see whether Paul, Abraham or possibly Solomon held the answer to such questions.

In due time, all three were married, with or without Solomon's help.

"But finding the right one can sometimes be as difficult as landing a space shuttle," said John Mayer, currently the world's best guitarist, on the TV show Skavlan.

Chapter 24

'Then Build Your Own Nursing Home, Jalle!'

Jarl Josefsson moved to Värnamo together with his family. At around the same time, Börje Kindström came to Värnamo without them knowing about each other. That was in the mid-1970s.

Jarl was an anesthetic nurse by profession and Börje was a physiotherapist. Both were involved in the Pentecostal congregation's youth work, and together, they started the Emigrants, a multi-active group of boys and girls. Their program included sports, hiking, skis, canoeing and Bible reading.

For me as an associate to pastor Tore Bengtsson, Jarl's and Börje's involvement was so positive. I did not have what it took myself to muster the imagination that such youth work requires. The congregation and the other committed leaders, as for example Karl-Erik Johansson and Stig Engvall, received the Josefsson's and Kindström's with open arms, and the youth work grew extensively, deep and wide.

They had a spiritual and practical foundation for this commitment with them from Filadelfia Stockholm, which is being recounted elsewhere in this book.

Jarl's and Börje's contacts with Lars Hörnberg had become sporadic. Lars Hörnberg was established as a well-known Pentecostal pastor and was working as a preacher in the Elim congregation in Malmö as Jack-Tommy Ardenfors's closest associate. Lars's wife Inga-Maj was recognized already at this time as a skilled soloist and guitarist. Who does not remember her Swedish translation of "Morning Has Broken"?

Then, the personal disaster for Inga-Maj and Lars Hörnberg struck. The divorce was a fact.

Inga-May saved her career, but Lars became unemployed. The pastoral ministry ceased, the telephone stopped ringing, and the colleagues were conspicuously absent. A pastor who had divorced had thus also disqualified himself both from ministry and the social pattern that the pastoral colleagues had created. For a while, Lars struggled to make ends meet, and ended his struggling career as a cleaner in Linköping's apartment block staircases.

It was in Linköping he met Linda Hutchens who was an evangelist in the Sion congregation there and a missionary to Romania. After the wedding, officiated by Alvar Henningsson, Linda and Lars were called to the Pentecostal church in Falköping. Pastor Christer Zethson and the congregation's elders dared to take the "risk" to call a previously divorced and remarried pastor to service. Honor to the congregation in Falköping!

In the early 1990s, Jarl Josefsson, together with his wife Margareta, had started a unique and successful career with building a number of nursing homes in the country. The career from start and until now is a real live success story. From his work as an anesthetic nurse via a long stint within the pharmaceutical industry, Jarl built the first nursing home in Norrtälje. That was soon followed by a number of similar plants, and the successful idea has not yet seen its end.

The start of Margareta's and Jarl's careers within the healthcare sector almost happened by coincidence, if you use common vocabulary and do not believe in God's guidance. As it happened, Margareta had promised to stand in for a nurse, but was prevented from that for one reason or another. Her husband, the anesthetic nurse Jarl, then offered his services, which was accepted.

Jarl came home from that work one day and had many opinions about what he had seen as an ordinary stand-in nurse at the ward. He was almost upset about one thing after another.

Margareta thought he was being negative and exclaimed: "Then build your own nursing home, Jalle!"

No sooner said than done! Immediately after that, Jarl incorporated a business together with a good friend. Capital stock at SEK 50,000 was now available, and with that sum as a foundation, he borrowed SEK 50 million at the bank! The municipality allocated a site, and a new and privately owned nursing home soon saw the light of day. That is apparently what can happen if you have the confidence of the municipality. At least that is how it could happen in the early 1990s.

Approximately 20 new nursing homes were quickly built across the country. It goes without saying that it took all spare time for the Josefsson family. The voluntary commitment to the congregation in Norrtälje did not suffer from the new things that were happening in Margareta's and Jarl's lives. Both one thing and another probably form the basis of what happened after that. These experiences laid the foundation for future events.

The devastating tsunami struck Asia and Thailand with full disastrous force.

The devastation and an enormous loss of life was a fact. The same morning, I was on my way to the Mission church in Reftele to preach, together with Gudrun and my daughter's family. It was on Boxing Day, 2004, when we could listen during our trip to the increasingly terrifying news reports from Thailand. The TV images later that day were surreal. No-one in my family had ever heard the word 'tsunami' and perhaps only a few Swedes had heard the word. Thailand, this friendly Siam with the friendly and smiling people with deep relations to Sweden through Swedish missionaries and later with millions of Swedish tourists, had been struck by an incomprehensible force of nature with devastating consequences for a long time to come.

A few weeks after the tsunami, I come out of the grocery store in Vetlanda, when the telephone rings. I am just about to shut the door of the car and drive home. "Hi, it's Jarl," the voice says. "Well hi there, long time no see!" After some small talk Jarl asks: "What are you doing nowadays, Roland? I suppose you're retired since a few years, right? But a guy like you can't reconcile with being retired and inactive, can you?"

"Ah, come on now Jarl, of course you understand that if you've been involved in Erikshjälpen for half a lifetime, you don't become idle as a pensioner."

But my reality was probably that I again was thinking about how long my life could be. After what the doctor had told me, I knew that it could end sooner than I had planned. 22 Twenty-two years earlier, I had had successful cancer surgery, but now my doctor had discovered metastases in my lungs, and perhaps my time on Earth would now come to its end after all. I had ended my commitment to the board of the Pentecostal church, the

Presidency of the Rotary club had ended, and the task as Assisting Governor was something I had handed over to a colleague.

When the doctor now gave me the shocking announcement, I openly went out and told about it. At the previous occasion 22 years earlier, I had thought that I would be able to keep my cancer secret, even to my wife and family. That had been a bad decision that I would deeply regret. So, this time, it was a self-evident opportunity to tell them. My wife Gudrun had been with me when the doctor informed me, and we sat at home in our living-room, crying.

"I never thought that the cancer would return," Gudrun cried. Nope who would have thought that. But now, it was a fact after all, and I told my Rotary club that it could withdraw my nomination for the position as Governor.

When Jarl called, I had gotten over the first year's pondering on the in-durability of life. Please note that I write "pondering" and no other dramatic concept. But apparently my enthusiastic voice did not sound the way I thought it would sound in Jarl's ears. He perceived me as somewhat disillusioned. And perhaps that was true. I had prayed to God for a new, solid task, and here, Jarl presented something beginning along those lines.

"What do we do with the consequences of the tsunami?" Jarl asked. "We can't just pretend nothing has happened. With the experience you have from Erikshjälpen, surely you'd be able to come up with some kind of proposal," he continued.

"Oh by the way, you're part of the international board of Caminul Felix, aren't you?" he said. "And by the way, have you heard anything about what Lars Hörnberg thinks about the matter? After all, he's been talking about there being millions of children being without a mom and dad in this world. Now, there are even more homeless and orphaned children in Phuket, Thailand."

"Yes, I'm on the board of Caminul Felix, and there, my old friend John Wildrianne from England is also a member, together with Peter Jenkins and an American named Bob Pagett, not to mention Berndt Sanfridson, and a few other friends from Sweden," I replied.

"Call Lars Hörnberg, Jarl," was my response.

Around this time, Jarl, Lars and Börje only knew about each other from a distance. Perhaps they had had some kind of contact with each other at one occasion or another. Of course, they had not been able to avoid reading about the preacher Lars Hörnberg, who apparently was back again after the divorce, had married Linda, and who sometimes toured Sweden with Romanian children's choirs.

That is how things went. Not only did Lars Hörnberg catch on at once, he and Linda had been thinking themselves along the same lines as Jarl.

Jarl, Berndt Sanfridson and I traveled to England and met with John Wildrianne and Peter Jenkins and Lars and Linda came from Romania. We worked enthusiastically for two days. We tossed ideas around, and in our imagination we opened many doors to Phuket in Thailand.

We delegated Jarl to become the coordinator, and he immediately wrote the first draft. After a few minor adjustments, we signed the letter of intent, which was to be presented to the authorities in Thailand, and to others who wanted to support us. He wrote it in an hour, and we now thought that it would work out with a nice project for the homeless of Phuket.

John Wildrianne and Peter Jenkins went to Phuket soon after that. They had a missionary colleague there, who would surely be able to show us where and how we would work. Linda and Lars also went there. Jarl Josefsson joined the group and contacts were established. The Wildrianne and Jenkins pastors and a missionary colleague invested huge financial resources in the area, summoned English financiers, and built a school.

But it would later turn out that Phuket and the people there were not the ones who needed our help. The relatively few children who had become orphaned in the tsunami were taken care of by relatives and by members of the royal family in Thailand.

Much later, when we had become established in Surat Thani, and half the family village had been erected, I got to speak on location to pastor K., who had been the main pastor of a congregation in Phuket for two periods, and then our goal became more clear. The thing was that many international organizations had rushed to Phuket, Kao Lak and other places stricken by the tsunami, he said. There was a virtual race to achieve something that could be showcased to the world. Congregations in Phuket, who had been contacted by International aid organizations, saw an increase in membership for a while, but after the aid had ceased or was no longer urgent, the number of members dropped again.

Building congregations was not Linda and Lars Hörnberg's first choice. The vision that they carried had the children as its first priority. That was the foundation on which Caminul Felix had been built. Building congregations was something other people could do.

The next meeting with Jarl, Lars and Linda took place at Yvonne and Lars-Åke Egerbo's home in Värnamo. They had been missionaries to the part of Asia which we had focused on.

We were thus quite a number of experienced and knowledgeable people meeting in Värnamo. I recall Lisa Egerbo being there as well. We then understood that our friends in England wanted to complete their mission in Phuket by themselves. A mission that the English were already underway carrying out without us and our participation, in spite of us, after all, being the ones coming up with the idea of a collaboration.

Jarl travelled to Thailand and established a contact with the missionary Görel Krohn, who knew the social situation well after many years in Thailand. Linda and Lars Hörnberg also travelled to Thailand and met with Görel Krohn and also with Eva Olofsson in Chiang Rai in northern Thailand. Eva had already started a project with AIDS-related children. Görel probably had this in mind and invited Lars to congregations in southern Thailand, including Surat Thani, where Lars presented his vision to the congregations that Görel collaborated with.

The vision that Linda and Lars carried was to provide vulnerable children with a new mother and a new father would not fail for Thai children now when there were no children from the tsunami available, so to speak. There were children who had experienced another terrible trauma. They had seen their parents die from AIDS, and relatives who were horrified and who had not dared to take on the little ones. They believed the risk of infection was too large.

Lars and Linda felt that the AIDS-related children in Surat Thani were calling for them. An inaudible but powerful "help us" cry was hurled into Lars's and Linda's consciousness and warm hearts.

Linda would not see the Felix Family Village come to

completion. The disease that she had struggled with for quite a long time struck again. She was admitted to a Budapest hospital, and soon, we realized that Linda would not win the fight for her life.

Jarl and his Margareta came over to Budapest with medicines and painkillers, but God took Linda home in August, 2005.

* * *

Linda's death shook us quite considerably. Linda grew up in a warm, Christian home in California. She studied at John Wildrianne's Bible School in Sussex, England. Missionary trips and experiences in Eastern Europe equipped her for much longer service in God's kingdom than she actually lived.

Lars remembered the time when everything had burst for him, when the painful divorce occurred, and there were no soft hands available in the Pentecostal movement when he would have needed them the most. He remembered how he was searching for the meaning of his life,; "the big purpose". When Linda came into his life, his life became whole again. Linda made his life complete and she became his beloved life companion. The vision had been birthed together, and was also carried together with Linda. Now, Linda was dead, and Lars had to carry on the vision himself. Not really by himself, for there were many collaborators within Caminul Felix who were raised up and they formed an efficient team to carry on the vision with renewed strength and the Vision gained new strength and grew further.

Linda had focused exclusively on the children's village Caminul Felix. She struggled and toiled for it to become as good as possible. When she realized that the disease would defeat her, she calmly discussed it through with the staff and the choir that she led: "It's soon time for me to move on, but when I go, you should know that I go to Jesus," she said, and was quoted by Carl-Henric Jaktlund in Dagen, the Christian daily.

Linda's calm before the inevitable end gave us all strength to continue to believe in a meaning of life, "the big purpose," as Lars put it. Linda wanted to plan parts of the forthcoming funeral service herself. A few weeks before the end, she suddenly called me with a strange request:

"Hi, Roland, I want you to play the trombone at my funeral," she said. I answered that I would of course try to fulfill her wish.

"Do you have any request for any particular music?" I asked Linda and probably expected her to request any of the usual funeral songs.

"Yes, I'd like you to play 'Oh, When The Saints Go Marching In...!'"

I gasped for breath! A valve trombone and this happy and rhythmical song at a funeral? "Yes, that's the way I want it," she said.

I played "Oh, When The Saints Go Marching In" on my trombone, and the 500 people attending sang with inspiration the well-known spiritual "Oh, Lord, I want to be in that number when the saints go marching in!"

Lars asked me to conduct Linda's graveside ceremony.

Linda is buried at Caminul Felix 2 in Oradea, Romania.

Chapter

25

Felix's Soccer Team

Pastor Mana Rujirayanyong met us at the airport at Surat Thani together with pastor K., or Ratchasak Pantasanya, which is his full name. The two pastors look like healthy young men, which they are, and a bit over 40 years old. We hardly were in the car before we started talking about two major topics; "What did you preach about last Sunday? and the joy of Christian soccer teams being formed in Thailand.

This is my first visit to Surat Thani and the Felix village. I have been able to follow the project all the way from start. I have seen pictures of the beautiful houses and I have heard of new mothers and fathers. I had followed the miracle from the beginning, I had taken part in planning and decisions that have been taken in faith that God would show his will and idea, and then the first conversation is about soccer!

Pastor Mana has been an assistant pastor to his father, who was the senior pastor of a small congregation in Surat Thani with about 40 members, for several years. Some time ago, they shifted things around, and now Mana is the senior pastor and his father is his associate.

Proudly, he tells us that, and outside his house in the Felix family village, the celebration flowers from the dedication in church are planted in large earthenware pots.

From the beginning of the construction of the Felix family village, Mana was involved. He speaks good English, and has studied the language in England for a whole year. Mana is the natural leader since the founder Lars Hörnberg and the board of Caminul Felix Sweden decided to start up in Thailand. Moreover, he is a member and secretary of the Thai Pentecostal movement, whose local congregation in Surat Thani was founded by Adolf Nilsson in the early 1950s.

From this Pentecostal congregation, a number of churches have emerged throughout town, all of which having their source in Adolf Nilsson. In the beginning, the spinoffs were painful, of course, but with the young pastors' broad-mindedness, the damage was now healed.

The earlier divisions were now only an annoying memory for the movement.

There are plans to build a temple with two thousand seats, where large services and conferences can be held in joint campaigns to evangelize Surat Thani.

Pastor Ratchasak Pantasanya – or Pastor K., which is much easier to pronounce, was a pastor in Phuket both before and after the tsunami hit the city with devastating force in 2004. He is, together with his wife, one of the new parent couples who head one of the houses that have been completed foe the AIDS-related children, as are pastor Mana and his wife.

Both pastors love sports, and especially soccer. Nurturing such interests beside the pastoral ministry has perhaps not always been looked upon favorably by some of the older people in the denomination. But here in Surat Thani, pastor K. as a soccer leader has managed to convince the doubting that it could lead to something good.

The model has been fetched from a Presbyterian pastor in Korea, who has been a missionary to Thailand for many years. Here, he has formed the Emanuel Football Club in Thailand. That happened already 11 years ago. His name is Mr. Kang Song Min, and he is proud to have his name in the Guinness Book of Records as the world champion of being able to keep a soccer ball in the air for 12 hours straight.

In Thailand, some 90 soccer clubs have been formed since then, but also in neighboring countries including Burma, Laos and Vietnam. All clubs have a Christian foundation. They argue is that the clubs could form a bridge for young people to reach other young people with the happy message of salvation. There have already been a few international matches against Laos and Vietnam. In an exhibition match between Korea and Thailand, senators from the Thai government formed the national team. How the match ended, I do not know.

One thing is stressed and that is that every match will begin in prayer with all players involved. Some of the young soccer players have already shown interest in church and regularly visit church. A few have even become Christians.

Emanuel Football Club has produced eight young men who now play for the Thai junior national team.

Observant news freaks will soon notice that the founder of the Emanuel Football Club, Mr. Kang Song Min, will be presented in a film which will be spread all over the world. He is already on YouTube.

In a few years, the Felix soccer club will be ready to represent the country, using soccer as a mighty weapon to spread the Gospel to the young Thai people.

Chapter 26

Missionaries from the Småland Bible Belt

Both Gunilla and Johan Akterhed came from the Bible belt area of Sweden, Småland. Gunilla's spiritual life was shaped by the Swedish Alliance Mission's congregation in Skärstad, and Johan by the Korskyrkan church in Aneby, which, in those days, belonged to the Örebro Mission.

Johan had studied to become an engineer, and worked at Hags in Aneby, which made playground equipment. The company is well known in many parts of the world. The company was started by the legendary missions man Rune Gustavsson, and was later run by the sons-in-law Bo Bauer and Sven-Åke Sjöstam. I had taught Sven-Åke to play the trumpet when we used to live in Hultsfred in the 1960s. There, in the small Pentecostal church in Hultsfred, was a brass band with 25 members, and Sven-Åke played first trumpet.

In other words, the conditions were good for Johan to become a missionary! Gunilla received an MBA degree, and her goal was to dedicate her life to business. Building her life on a Christian basis, making good deals and earn a lot of money simply could not be wrong, she believed.

So far, Johan and Gunilla did not know about each other. Johan took time off from Hags and spent a few months in Thailand with Youth With A Mission. With his appetite for missions whetted, he returned to Sweden, met Gunilla, and then things happened the way they happened; love, engagement and matrimony.

However, there would be no wedding until Gunilla could try out life as a YWAMer, Johan argued. Even though she liked business the spreading of the Kingdom of God should be considered a first priority in life. Then, all the other things could come in rapid succession, wedlock and common interests. That was more or less what Jesus had said himself, the author of missions, wasn't it?

Gunilla then travelled to Ethiopia and then to Thailand and Australia together with Johan. There, they tried life as the messengers of Christ or as YWAMers, that is, if there is any difference.

Returning home again, Gunilla and Johan Akterhed continued their careers, until they one day were told what Lars Hörnberg was doing in Thailand.

Berndt Sanfridson and Johan Akterhed, who belonged to the same congregation in Aneby, had discussed missions with each other many times over the years. The conferences at Ralingsås nearby, where inspired missionaries challenged the crowds, played a large role in Johan's life.

In Berndt's case, a thought was developing. Perhaps Johan and Gunilla were suited to be part of the team that was to realize the Felix Family Village (FFV) in Surat Thani and give the planned family village the content that had proven so successful in Romania?

At a Felix board meeting in Aneby, their names came up. Berndt Sanfridson was given the task to check with Gunilla and Johan. Perhaps our interest in them came as a bit of a surprise for them at that moment after all. Both of them have good jobs, Gunilla was quite happy with her work, and Johan had advanced to Vice President of the company and was very happy.

"When we had finally decided to take the challenge to become missionaries in Thailand, everything went ahead at breakneck speed," says Johan. "We could wind down our commitments in Sweden without any real problems. Gunilla was able to take a leave from work, and I could step down from my position in a good way. It seemed as though we were going into what the old-time Christians used to call 'good works before ordained'," Johan concludes.

"The Filadelfia Church in Stockholm with Gunnar Swahn and Karl-Johan Winberg and in Huddinge stitched together a so-called mini project that fit the entire setup for our PMU commitment to

Johan Akterhed, Berndt Sanfridson, Roland Nelsson and Gunilla Akterhed at Elsies Café in Nässjö.

Surat Thani in Thailand," John continues his story.

"The PMU and SIDA (The Swedish International Development Cooperation Agency) wanted to go for an HIV/AIDS project and that suited me very well. I acquired some basic knowledge at SIDA's school in Härnösand, and when we came out to Surat Thani, I and the Thais put together a project description anchored in eleven of the Thai Pentecostal movement's congregations in the

South. The aim was to educate the Thai and provide important knowledge about HIV/AIDS."

Johan believes that he has been able to fulfill the project and that it is now moving along by its own power in the eleven congregations. From there, other congregation and community fellowships will be able to take part in acquiring this knowledge.

It is now Twelfth Night, 2010, and we are sitting at Elsie's Café in Nässjö, telling each other about God's ways with our lives. Gunilla and Johan have completed their term as missionaries to Thailand after two years. Their son Noah, soon eight years old, is with them at the café and for a few hours he is content with listening to the adults' experiences in Thailand. Noah is enterprising, however, and is getting to know other guests at the café. He will surely become a great missionary in time!

Outside, it is -12C below zero, and the snow lies in huge drifts outside the café window. After an excursion across the café's premises, Noah is back, announcing that in Phuket, you could bathe in the sea every day during the time the family lived there. "There, in Phuket, there was both a Swedish and an International school," he said. Of course, he was very happy there, and speaks English just like any little Englishman. Linn, who is six years, and Emelie, who was born in Thailand and is 20 months old, are being babysat at home in Jönköping while we are talking away a few hours at Elsie's Café.

I, for one, remember with inspiration the conferences we used to have at the Rörstrand in Stockholm together with Gunnar Swahn and Karl-George Winberg.

Hosting the Temple meeting in Filadelfia was Jarl Josefsson with his wife Margareta. It was just after New Year, 2007, and before everything had actually happened. Lars Hörnberg presented the concept that he had carried as a vision for many years, and which had proven not only feasible in Romania, but which had also changed the official view of children in the country that the Ceausescu regime had so maliciously been exploiting.

The two representatives of the Swedish Pentecostal mission, Gunnar Swahn and Karl-George Winberg, believed that a similar concept could be feasible also in Thailand, and they wanted to help us.

Such a positive attitude from the Pentecostal movement's representatives was something completely new to me. If Caminul Felix had existed in the 1980s, it would have been called a para church organization without any chance of collaboration with the Pentecostal mission.

Retentive readers know, for example, that great organizations such as Erikshjälpen and Elida had indeed been portrayed as para church organizations.

In those days they only wanted to support and safeguard what had emanated from the Pentecostal movement, that is, the many common companies.

I recall, for example, how mighty men from the Movement discussed with SIDA about not supporting Erikshjälpen with project money that Erikshjälpen sometimes applied for. SIDA's own representatives soon afterwards gave us detailed accounts about the meeting that the denominational leaders had called, and snorted at their nonsense.

Gunilla, Emelie, Johan, Linn and Noah Akterhed

Another example can be mentioned. My organization, Erikshjälpen, could not advertise in the Dagen daily as we were not exclusively a Pentecostal company. This ban ceased after a while when Dagen's director Sverre Larsson realized the absurdity in the ban and personally headed a natural change.

Sverre Larsson has played a role in realizing FFV in Surat Thani that was not insignificant. As chairman of the board of the newspaper Världen idag, he suggested that the paper's readers would be offered a chance to finance building one of the ten houses in the village. Today, the house proudly stands there, with a sign on the fasade showing who had paid for the building.

Now, perhaps you, dear reader, would argue that what has just been recalled in my memory here does not belong to this story. But I just wanted to show that times change, organizations' and movements' teething problems can be cured, and that the agents of health sooner or later get the opportunity to carry out what the Lord has called them to do. Gunilla and Johan Akterhed are good representatives here for a changed attitude from the religious world around them.

So now, this was 2007, and our friends Gunnar Swahn and Karl-George Winberg opened up for Caminul Felix establishing in Thailand. That was something that not only the "brethren" from Stockholm did, but Caminul Felix immediately became a participant in the annual country consultations within the Pentecostal movement concerning the missions and aid work in Thailand.

Upon the inauguration of the Family Village in Surat Thani in the spring of 2009, the Swedish Pentecostal movement was represented by pastor Görgen Hellman and Eva Jansson from the missions committee in Vetlanda.

"So suddenly, we found ourselves in Surat Thani," Gunilla exclaims where we sit at Elsie's Café in Nässjö on this cold and wintery day in January, 2010. "I suppose we had some homesickness with us in our baggage for the first few days. My being full-term pregnant probably contributed to my homesickness. But to my relief, a team of Swedes headed by pastor Görgen Hellman came to visit right at that moment. We hit it off very well.

If only you knew how much easier it made my introduction to the country!" says Gunilla. "Even though both Johan and I had studied Thai already in Sweden, just being able to speak Swedish with a Swedish midwife, well, that meant very much. God was good to me!"

Johan had been given the task by the PMU to write a plan of action for an HIV/AIDS project which would be implemented in a number of Pentecostal congregations, as mentioned.

The board and Berndt Sanfridson holding the just obtained documents stating Felix Villages the new owners of the land in Surat Thani.

Gunilla was given the task to become the FFV's Swedish representative. Johan was being paid by PMU and good supporters and friends ensured that Gunilla also received financial aid. It goes without saying that the tasks wove into one another for Gunilla and Johan.

It was important that Gunilla was part of the initial phase to sketch out what reality would look like in a few years. Johan was included in that picture as far as his time allowed him. At a previous visit, Berndt Sanfridson had, together with the Thai leaders, chosen the site that the Felix Family Village would be built on. The site was paid for with donated funds from Sweden. To an outside observer, the site looked like it was impossible to build houses upon. It is located in the river delta and was offered by a couple of elderly ladies for its ratable value.

The site is 2 1/2 hectares. In fact, the whole of Surat Thani is

The newly bought land for the Felix Village in Surat Thani.

The land full of soil to be built on.

The first houses under construction.

built on a river delta, a mangrove swamp. Finding another suitable site at a reasonable price was hardly possible.

After several thousand truck loads, the wetland had been filled up to solid ground, and the foundations for the houses were laid.

It was of utmost importance that the Akterhed's were involved from the beginning in selecting house parents and in the educational seminars that were arranged. Even though Johan had his main mission in the eleven congregations with his HIV/AIDS project, his knowledge was also of importance in the family village's seminars. After all, the children in the village were fetched from AIDS-related family situations.

Perhaps one or both parents had died from AIDS and the children's relatives would not consider such a child. They were usually left to their own fate.

Jonas Adolfsson from Världen idag cut the ribbon to the "Världen idag-house."

I will not go into detail here into Thailand's HIV/AIDS problems. Just a few pieces of information that illustrate the matter.

Out of more than 65 million inhabitants, more than 600,000 are infected with the disease, of which 14,000 are children, but there is probably a large number of hidden statistics as well.

HIV infection is most widespread in northern Thailand close to the Golden Triangle, because of opium and intravenous drug use in the area. Northern Thailand also has the highest concentration of HIV subtype B.

About 80% of those infected with HIV are heterosexuals, compared with about 10% in the U.S. and other Western countries.

It is thus known to us, who have somewhat understood the

Margareta and Jarl Josefsson cut the band to"their" house.

children's traumatic situation, that relatives do not absorb the children into the community when the parents have died from AIDS.

That is also what the missionary Görel Krohn, who has a long experience from social/evangelic work in Thailand, says. The fear of HIV is great, and people believe that they can be infected simply by being near such a child.

Both Johan's and Gunilla's efforts are invaluable, and now, as the couple have left their mission field in Thailand after two years, the projects with the AIDS programs are completed.

Their work has been founded on knowledge and practical work and love for the new village's families.

"Our primary commitment has been consultative and of an advisory nature," Gunilla and Johan Akterhed say. "The Thai leadership needs support in the future as well. They have grown

The five first Felix-couples in front of their new houses.

a lot and have practiced 'learning by doing' during the two years that lie behind. Our confidence in them is high," the Akterhed's conclude their analysis.

Eight houses have thus been erected with funds from Sweden and the U.S. and also a Community Center, where larger gatherings can take place. There is also an exhibition hall for products that have been made either in the family village or in its vicinity. Guests staying overnight also find a couple of guest rooms. In the building, there is also an operation room which can be adapted to any medical needs that may arise in the family village.

One of the houses has been paid for by the newspaper Världen idag, which raised the money among its readers, something that was initiated by the paper's chairman, Sverre Larsson. A beautiful sign telling about the gift from Världen idag's readers decorates the front of the house. On another house, I can see the names

Jarl Josefsson and Mana Rujirayanyong

Margareta and Jarl Josefsson as donors. One erected house has been financed by a family in Småland. Its plaque will decorate the house they have financed. A good friend of Caminul Felix in USA, Jim Sankey, has donated good amounts of money for our ministries, including houses in Thailand.

The Open Hand store in Nyköping has, for many years, been a supporter of the Felix concept. The Open Hand store donated large sums already when the second family village in Romania was being built. A decision has now been made to also finance one of the forthcoming five houses in Thailand.

The site has generous proportions, and so another two houses have been planned. In front of the completed houses, a lawn, flowers, and bushes grow. At the back, towards the canal, vegetable cultivation is already underway. When the other houses will be built, a green open space and a soccer field and playground will decorate the compound's center.

120 children will then get a safe childhood and adolescence together with the ten house parent couples who have dedicated their lives to shaping an entire generation.

Lisa Egerbo travels to Thailand every now and then and Lars Hörnberg regularly comes to the seminars. Jarl Josefsson showed incredible interest in the project from the very beginning.

Actually, it was Jarl who put us on the right track from the very first beginning. It was soon after the tsunami in 2004 and which I have told about in another chapter. He had experience from the Philippines, where he had been the director of the Scandinavian Children's Mission (Skandinaviska Barnmissionen) which had originally been started by the legendary variety artist and later missionary Sigvard Wallenberg. Jarl also had the financial resources for costs that arose in the initial phase.

Here, it might be appropriate to remind you of the gigantic labor that the office in Aneby has invested in the implementation of all the thoughts and ideas that came up in our meetings during the first few years after 2006. The protocols that are available to read from the first few years meetings bear witness to an intellectual commitment, combined with much written text.

For example; How contacts were being sought, what the arrangement between Filadelfia Stockholm and the PMU and the FFV would look like, how the contact between the Akterhed missionaries and the Thai collaborators would be arranged practically, about long and recurring telephone or Skype calls, about how foundations would be registered, which Swedish and international people beside the Thai who would have a seat and vote in the foundations, what the houses in Surat Thani would look like and which construction material should be used.

The first houses in the i Felix Village.

Discussions on how to reach the AIDS related children, selecting a father and a mother for each house unit, about administration and financial flow, communication with sponsors, etc. etc.

The spider in the web was and is Berndt Sanfridson, who, together with his wife Elise and the co-worker Ann-Marie Bauer, work faithfully and with great eagerness in the Swedish office.

Moreover, Berndt is chairman of the Swedish foundation and chief administrator. His hospital stay a few years ago because of a heart attack was short, and his return to work went smoothly.

The Felix village is based on sponsor systems. Individual people in Sweden promise to contribute a monthly sum for a shorter or longer period of time. "The sponsors are the most loyal supporters within the foreign aid sphere," Berndt Sanfridson says. "Nothing compares to their regular donations. This is worth gold and cannot be appreciated enough!"

But private donors in Surat Thani as well have understood the value of supporting the Felix village financially. The money is being conveyed via a few churches in town.

Sponsors living in the immediate vicinity of the family villages is a good sign. That shows that the Felix concept has been well thought through, and that it gains confidence among those who have experience and insight in the daily work for many years themselves.

At Caminul Felix in Romania, several of our house parents and older adolescents, who have moved out from their families, have stepped in as sponsors for the children in Thailand.

Chapter 27

The Parents at the Felix Family Village

You have come with me on the voyage to Surat Thani. We have already been here in another chapter in the book and I have outlined the background as to how the idea for the project came about. You have come with me into the lads' prayer meetings in Filadelfia Stockholm and seen how those meetings got to play a crucial role for the Felix Family Village in Thailand to come true.

Now, we are back there again, after looking into the mirrors of memory, and we have now driven onto the cement-clad road that meanders past the five houses on the left side of the road.

Within a near future, a community center needs to be built on this side of the road. The idea with this chapter is to try to portray the people who have become the new parent couples of the village. It is interesting to look into their personalities and understand how life has shaped them for their mission.

Suphot and Wiparat Junton in House 1

We stop by at the first house, which was completed by March, 2010. A couple from Småland has paid for the cost of the project, SEK 750,000. It is the fifth house to come into use. Eventually, another five houses will be built at the opposite end of the site as soon as the financing is available. When the village is completed, 120 children will live here together with ten parent couples.

The two new parents have already been appointed, and are now waiting eagerly to move in with their four children. Right now, they are renting an apartment downtown with the Felix spirit in their hearts.

Their names are Suphot and Wiparat Junton, both 39 years old, and they have two children of their own, eight and six years old, and two Felix children.

Suphot and Wiparat Junton

Suphot comes from an old Christian family. Faith in God goes way back in the family. Suphot's parents were not affluent, and they were often given financial support by foreign missionaries in order to survive. A Danish missionary meant quite a lot to the family, and Suphot's younger brother was adopted away in Denmark and married a Danish girl. The brother was a surviving twin. The twin brother had died at birth. The surviving brother had major heart problems and that was the reason why he was adopted away to Denmark.

For as long as he can remember, Suphot has nourished a yearning to serve God and to have his life well-planned. If I tell you that Suphot already at age nine had appointed Wiparat as his future wife and that he prayed for this every day until the wedding, you will understand, dear reader, that Suphot is a man of visions that he realizes.

They had met during their teenage years a bit at a distance at youth camps, but the intended wife did not seen to be too interested.

Eventually, Suphot ended up as a banker in Bangkok. Wiparat had also moved to Bangkok and found a job within telecommunications. It was here in Bangkok that they met each other again, and now, Wiparat finally became interested in the lad who had prayed so eagerly for God to give him her and no one else for a wife.

Many years later, the future wife Wiparat had heard about the brother with the large heart defect who had been adopted away. It was during the days in her youth when she worked among abandoned children that the Pentecostal church in Surat Thani was responsible for.

Then, Lars Hörnberg arrives to the congregation in Surat

Lars Hörnberg

Thani, informing about the planned project, the Felix Family Village. It is the missionary Görel Krohn who has invited Lars to the congregations in Surat Thanu. Suphot and Wiparat are present in church, listening to Lars. Well, Suphot probably thought that what Lars is on fire for is probably good, and Lars's vision could surely be realized, but as for myself, I am probably too old for such things, he thought. Secondly, it is not conceivable that a man would take care of other people's children.

Moreover, his mother probably was not too pleased about the idea.

But a film on TV about the orphans and a nightly dream changed everything. They perceived the two events as a message from God, and now, they are happy parents both of their own and of others people's children. Now, they are only waiting for the house to be completed. Many AIDS related and orphaned children are waiting for their new Mum and Dad.

Ataya and Wallee Noamai in House 2

Ataya Noamai is 54 years old and his wife Wallee Noamai is 44.

The have two children of their own, 23 and 21 years old. Five years ago, they adopted a girl who is now 21 years old. That adoption took place long before the family village was even planned.

When Ataya was in his 20s, he established a kindergarten for children between two and six years old. He had grown up in a nominally Christian home. His father was a carpenter and the family lived as Christians in name only.

In the kindergarten, the teachers played forth their teaching in subjects that are common in similar Buddhist preschools. But

Ataya and Wallee Noamai

since he had had a Christian upbringing, it was natural to play forth the knowledge of an Almighty God as well. Perhaps not all parents liked the Christian elements in the kindergarten. After all, Buddhism does not have any almighty god to worship.

When he met his future wife about 24 years ago and started a family, he felt God telling him very clearly to build his family with responsibility and faith in God. His own children would be able to grow up with a father and a mother who could thank God for their family and for a warm, Christian home.

Just before their marriage, a tragic car accident occurred, caused by his inattention, and an elderly woman was killed. It happened in the school yard and was witnessed by several hundred people. Ataya was plagued by recurring nightmares for a long time. In that situation, being severely depressed, he finally met a pastor who could pray for him.

The nightmares disappeared immediately, and it was then that he changed his nominal Christian life into a life that would be Christ-like.

As the Felix village then started being discussed, they felt that God was calling them to step into the Felix family concept.

Wallee Noamai's family were Buddhists. Her father, who was a policeman, was a drinker, and her home was a place of discontent and loud arguments. In the vicinity were Christian youth who prayed for the young people on the block.

They took Wallee with them to the church nearby and she started attending regularly on Sundays. Eventually, she realized that there must be a God – Buddhists do not believe in any god – and one Saturday, a spiritual wrestle started that lasted until the next morning when there was a service in church. She was then 17 years old, and that morning, she met the Almighty.

Both of them went into higher education, Ataya training to become a teacher and Wallee to become an accountant, and both of them worked in Bangkok.

It was at a Christian camp building that the two of them would later meet. Both of them were committed believers, and understood that the Lord had a plan with their life together.

Lars Hörnberg was invited to Surat Thanu, and held a seminar in a church and Atala and Wallee had been invited. At the seminar, Lars taught about the divine project that had won respect with the general public and with authorities in Romania. The concept was to build a family village where abandoned and AIDS related children could have a new home, a new Dad, and a new Mom. It did not take long until they understood that this was where the route for their commitment went. After all, they had already tried the adoption idea with their adoptive daughter, and now, they were ready to become parents for a rising generation.

Mana and Janyarak Rujirayanyong in House 3

This is where the leader of the Felix Family Village in Surat Thani lives, Mana Rujirayanyong with his wife Janyarak. There being a Felix family village in Surat Thani at all is mostly thanks to the missionary Görel Krohn. At another place in this book, I describe the events in our lives that just led our steps to Surat Thani.

Görel Krohn was the Swedish Pentecostal Mission's representative in Thailand, and was of incredible help when we were trying to find the location for our project, and the concept that had won so much respect in Romania, England, the U.S., Norway, Australia, just to mention a few of the countries that Caminul Felix has a

Mana and Janyarak Rujirayanyong

deep relation with. And who in Sweden has not heard of Caminul Felix, Linda and Lars Hörnberg, and Lisa Egerbo?

It was thus Surat Thani and pastor Mana who came into focus for the Felix idea thanks to Görel Krohn.

Brother Mana is a dynamic and prominent personality, with a great sense of humor, full of integrity, and the only one of the house parents who currently speaks English. But that is to be remedied now. Mana has started an English course where all house parents are welcome to come and learn. All house parents are in on the idea. On Wednesdays, a few hours are being set aside for learning English, which apparently very few Thai speak. Mana lived for a year in England, and thus has no problems with the language. Mana will also be helped by a couple of English teachers from Sweden.

Mana is on the Thai Pentecostal movement's board, is its secretary, and is well-informed about what happens within the country but also Internationally.

Mana is now the senior pastor of the small Pentecostal church in Surat Thani. He has succeeded his father, who is now Mana's collaborator.

When Mana was about 18 years old, his entire family was saved. His family owned the largest construction company in Surat Thani when both his parents were hit by deadly diseases. His mother, for some reason, became completely paralyzed, and his father was hit by liver cancer. His father, who had been a Buddhist monk for 10 years, died and preparations for the end were being made. But then he became saved on his death bed, and lives on, and has since then has been the senior pastor of the congregation until now when his son took over. His mother was also the subject of heavy intercession around this time. People gathered around her bed and prayed throughout the night. They interspersed the prayers with inspiring testimonies about what God can do, and they sang the right and inspiring worship songs, and in the morning, his mother had recovered completely.

The large construction firm was closed at the right moment in the 1990s. Worse times for companies hit Thailand, and many other companies went bankrupt.

Mana started a kindergarten downtown, and hired his wife as its principal. At the moment, they have three employees, and some 20 children in the kindergarten. The congregation pays the costs, and the municipality also contributes. The wife, Janyarak, has been working at the kindergarten without pay since its beginning.

It is their congregation that recruits new children for the kindergarten. She is still the one ultimately in charge, but much responsibility has been transferred to the employees in order for Mana and Janyarak to be able to spend their time on the FFV.

Janyarak was born in northern Thailand to Buddhist parents, and she is the only one in her family who has so far become a Christian. Janyarak is 45 years old and a mother of four. The children are seventeen, sixteen, fourteen and nine years old. There is also a Felix son who is 11 years old.

The school that Janyarak attended as a child was, of course, Buddhist. However, there was a Catholic female teacher in school, who dared to cross herself every now and then in front of the children. That awoke Janyarak's interest in Christian faith. When she later met Mana during her university education, where both of them studied the same subject, that is, computer skills, it did not take long until she accepted Jesus as her personal Savior and became Mana's wife.

Saksit and Sopit Kulsiripaiboom in House 4

We are sitting on the porch on typical Thai porch furniture. They have been carved into armchairs from some sort of high-grade wood with large, imaginary wheels, varnished with clear varnish, but are hardly comfortable. But the climate is wonderful. It is November, partially overcast and about +28 C and windless.

This was the second house to be built, as far as I can remember. Four houses have already been built, furnished, and inhabited. The fifth house will soon be completed. Sturdy houses were designed by a Thai architect and adjusted by

Jarl Josefsson. The house has two levels. The first floor is where the children live with the girls in one half and the boys in the other half. There is plenty of space from the first floor to the ceiling of the house. The roof has been built in two sections, one roof above the other, with an air gap in between. The idea is called "the

Saksit och Sopit Kulsiripaiboom

chimney effect" which means natural and continuous circulation of air. However, the rain cannot come in.

The alternative is an electric air conditioning unit, which both costs money to buy and is expensive to run. The staircase down from the dormitory areas, which have three toilets and showers each, is divided by a robust iron fence that separates the girls' area from the boys'. The ground floor contains a kitchen and a dining hall as well as a living room and offices and bedrooms for the parents. Outside the kitchen, there is a so-called "outdoors kitchen", as well as dishwasher and washing machine under an extending roof.

Just below the house, there is irregular vegetation that separates the narrow garden from a canal that is sometimes being used by the inhabitants of the house. All five houses look the same and all are located along the canal.

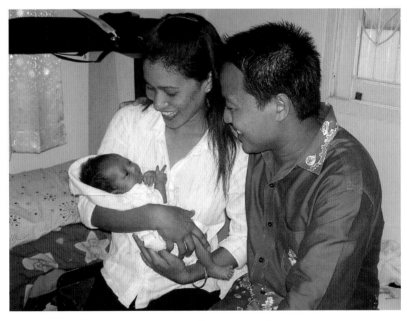

Saksit och Sopit tillsammans med Ettan.

In this house, Saksit and Sopit Kulsiripaiboom, both 40 years old, are the parents.

"Which background for this work do you have, Saksi?" I ask, and his response surprises me. "Well, I grew up as an orphan boy at the Asian Outreach International," he says. "That is a missions organization which is represented here and there all over Asia, with its headquarters in Hong Kong."

His answer stirs up memories in me. Surely Erikshjälpen had had some collaboration with that organization.

"I recall my organization, Erikshjälpen, having a project together with Asian Outreach International," I say. "I'm quite sure that it was in Chang Rai in northern Thailand. I remember the director there after a visit I paid many years ago. His name was Dr. Sombat." "Exactly," Saksit exclaims. "That's where I grew up as an orphan boy!"

Now, the former orphan boy is himself a father in house number four. The circle has been closed. He has grown up in a similar environment, and that is where he wanted to continue to work when he became an adult. That is a good grade for Asian Outreach International and Dr. Sombat. Perhaps not all orphanage institutions have the same results as Dr. Sombat has.

The concept that Lars Hörnberg introduced with the creation of Caminul Felix in Romania took into consideration the knowledge of how hard it is to raise children in institutions. The state institutions in Romania had been laid bare in their most hideous forms. That is not to say that all types of institutions would be complete failures, but the Felix concept is unbeatable with its idea of a new mother and a new father. The concept is spreading throughout the world through Lars Hörnberg's many International connections. Lars Hörnberg does not hesitate to inform about the incredible need for spreading parental love for the millions of homeless children worldwide. Each and every of them needs a new mother and a new father.

Lars usually takes Jesus' parents as an example. They were adoptive parents of the Son of God, Jesus.

Sopit and Saksit themselves carried a tragedy, they could not have children of their own, and only those who are in or have been in a similar situation know what that means.

Sopit and Saksit became the first ones to adopt a little newborn girl whom nobody wanted. The eleven-year-old mother of the girl had been raped by her 15-year-old brother. The 11-year-old had no idea why her belly grew bigger, and the delivery almost became a surprise to her. When the girl had been born, the new grandmother rejected her grandchild. Get her out! The hospital discouraged Saksit and Sopit from adopting the child for it did not seem to be completely healthy. But the girl's little eyes looked up at them, almost pleading.

They could not defend themselves from the feeling that it was their own child yearning for them. Sopit and Saksit received the little child, who was named Ettan.

A couple of Swedish volunteers thought that the name was suitable as it was the first child to arrive at the Felix family village.

The announcement came that now all adoption papers have been completed and Ettan is now your child.

The same day the announcement came, Ettan died. She had developed cancer in her head, and there was nothing to do. Ettan was buried in an extensive and dignified manner. She was then given a new, posthumous name by her grieving parents, Emerald, which is the name of a highly valued gem.

Now, Sopit and Saksit are waiting to have the house filled

with lively children. They have four children now, but there will eventually be twelve children in the house! "Ettan" in Swedish means "the Number One."

The adoption process was begun. It took time, and Ettan was 10 months old when previously been working as a deacon in a Pentecostal church, and Saksit has the experience from his time as an orphanage boy in Chiang Rai.

Ratchasak and Sirirat Pantasanya in House 5

This is where Pastor K. lives with his wife Sirirat Pantasanya. Of course, Pastor K. has a full name, Ratchasak Pantasanya, but for reasons easily understood, he is being addressed by the letter K. That is how things are done in the Felix village, and he is also known by that letter among the Swedes who have a relation with the village or within the mission.

Ratchasak och Sirirat Pantasanya

His wife, Sirirat, is seemingly the ruler of the house. Her eyes sparkle with a sense of humor, and she is quick-witted. As a child, Sirirat and her siblings studied the Bible successfully, and Sirirat eventually became her father's co-worker in a congregation in Surat Thani, teaching Sunday Schools and youth groups.

Missionary Jörgen Algesund ran a Bible School close by, and there, Sirirat later became a student for a period of time.

Sirirat and K. have two children of their own and five Felix children. The idea is that all the children are to feel the same security as their own biological children, not only for a short period of time, but forever. That is what the concept for Caminul Felix in Romania is like. The concept was given in a vision to the Hörnbergs more than 24 years ago. In Romania, the first generation's children are leaving their safe homes after 18 years since the beginnings in 1992. One good example of which there are several, is Eli and Marcel Filip, who have raised some 15 children in their house. Eli and Marcel are now leaving their house in the family village after all these years and have built their own house in Oradea.

All the children have been given an education and moved away from home. Some have even started their own families, and Eli and Marcel have become grandparents. There are birthdays, weddings and baptisms for the grandchildren. The family is becoming big!

One of the sons in Pastor K.'s house plays the saxophone, and is visiting good friends in Phuket during my visit. Phuket is on the West side, straight across from Surat Thani, and about 3 hours' drive away.

K. proudly shows me his son's saxophone, a new and solid instrument, and definitely of the kind of second-hand instruments that I learned to play on more than 60 years ago. It will be great fun to follow the lad's musical career.

K. is, together with Mana, the family village's natural leader. As Saksit in the neighboring house, K. grew up at an orphanage, but a Buddhist one. His parents got divorced when he was three months old, and his mother remarried. He no longer fit into his mother's new world, so therefore, she sent him to the temple so that the monks would take care of him.

In the temple, he was being raised a novice, but nobody could keep him from meeting other children outside the limits of the temple, and at age nine, he met a lad who was a Christian. That encounter resulted in him leaving the temple four years later and moving in with a Baptist family. However, his relation with his biological mother had not been completely broken, but K. visited his mother every now and then.

K. eventually became a Baptist pastor, and later, pastor of a Presbyterian congregation. He met Mana 21 years ago in Surat Thani. Mana was, at that time, his father's co-worker in the Pentecostal church, and soon afterwards, K. also became a Pentecostal pastor.

But during an interlude, K. also found time to try life as a cowboy on a large ranch run by the Church of God. Equipped not only with a lasso but also with a revolver and a rifle, he became a menace to mafia figures who disrupted order at the 320,000 square meter ranch.

Once, the mafia had kidnapped 15 cows, and demanded a large sum of money as a ransom. Equipped with his weapons, he and a co-worker fired around wildly. The cows regained their freedom and the mafia men took off, some injured but none killed.

With that experience from the Church of God, K. has been

named the Felix Family Village's snake killer. So far, two cobras, who have come too close to the village's houses, have been executed by K.'s trident fish spear with sharp flukes. I see the weapon standing ready for use in a corner of the kitchen, and later, I take a picture of K. and Mana with cowboy hats, cowboy boots and the important weapon. When we are standing talking outside one of the houses, we discover a beautiful snake, shimmering of green, in one of the bushes near the terrace. Jarl Josefsson is ready with his weapon, the camera, and moves closer to get a good picture.

At the speed of lightning, the snake pours down from the bush and across the yard and up into a tree close by. Soon enough, a mouse comes down from the tree, and is being hunted down by the snake, which coils its body around its prey. Jarl is now again ready with his camera, where the mouse is struggling for its life. The snake discovers Jarl, lets go of its prey, and disappears up the tree again. That resulted in some fine pictures by a surprised photographer.

"That was nice of you, Jarl, to save the mouse," said Lars Hörnberg.

Chapter
28

Sponsors

Elise and Berndt Sanfridson have, in a few years, built a nationwide sponsoring network in Sweden. Their office is in Aneby, housed in a charming building clad with gray brick. The building is actually an old factory building that used to be owned by the legendary missionary man Rune Gustavsson, the founder of the Kronoberg Mission (Kronobergsmissionen) and also one of the instigators of the conference center at Ralingsås.

Elise Sanfridson

Berndt Sanfridson

For a while, Berndt Sanfridson owned the KM-förlaget publishing house, and as a publisher, he has been involved in many titles, as for example Roberth Johansson's "Humor in Holy Chapels" ("Humor i helgade hyddor").

Elise and Berndt Sanfridson have a thorough education and a wide experience of missions at its best. From the middle of the 1980s, the Sanfridson spouses were the Örebro Mission's missionaries to Bangladesh and Thailand.

In his missionary task, Berndt served as a field secretary and representative of the mission to the state authorities. The position also meant keeping in touch with his missionary colleagues and collaboration organizations in parts of Asia, which meant many and long journeys across the borders.

After many years in Asia, the Sanfridson's established themselves in Aneby in 1994, and have now built an impressive sponsoring network called Svenska Barnhjälpen (The Swedish Children's Aid). A large number of sponsors send their money through them to Bangladesh.

Pastor Sven Larqvist and the Pentecostal congregation in Aneby had, through their missionaries Gunnel and Lennart Englund, a standing commitment to Argentina for many years. The work was carried out through the foundation Mi Casita (My Little House) which had been formed for the purpose. Its program included widespread sponsoring activities.

As time went on, there were a few staff changes within the Pentecostal congregation, which contributed to the Sanfridson's being offered to take over responsibility for Mi Casita.

So, on the charming old gray brick building's fasade in Aneby, three signs are now hanging. On these, you read, Svenska

Barnhjälpen, Mi Casita, and Caminul Felix, burnt in handwriting on pinewood from Småland.

Elise and Berndt are, in other words, no nestlings for they have taken on the task of great responsibility to convey gifts and sponsorship money to Caminul Felix in Oradea and to Surat Thani in Thailand. In just a few years, the network has grown from zero to more than a thousand sponsors. Every month, the sponsors send their support to children in Asia and Romania and Argentina.

Elise and Berndt believe that the sponsorship system is indeed the best way for families and individuals in Sweden to safely contribute to countries' social development.

Berndt puts it like this: "The sponsors are the most faithful supporters within the foreign aid sphere. Nothing compares to their regular donations. Every month, they send their money, year in and year out. This is worth gold and cannot be appreciated enough!"

Most often, well, always, the children that are most in need are the ones who become the subject of the sponsors' care and faithfulness. Without their support each month, the children would never have a chance of an education, perhaps not even an opportunity to get the most necessary things, such as food and clothes.

The sponsors' monthly support means continuity that nothing else can match. Every day, week, and month, food, shelter, and heat are of course needed. So-called spot grants from aid organizations, SIDA or governments, could provide the children with a school building, a library and medical facilities, but can never replace the warm attitude and the emotions that the sponsors' support provide," says Berndt Sanfridson.

Sponsorship is in vogue. A large number of such organizations exist in our country. Swedes are very aware of the sponsorship's excellent qualities. During the last few years, the media and celebrities have focused on sponsored children. "I have the child I sponsor in Cambodia," says Carola , for instance. Many other celebrities have followed her example.

Swedish TV has coined the concept of "Children of the World", and one of the TV channels have a sponsor's gala every fall. Hundreds of millions of crowns reach the children of the world in that very way. Not to mention Queen Silvia's organization for children in need.

"But," says Berndt, "the sponsoring activities that are being distributed through the Christian mission has a great advantage, that is, the low administration costs.

Those who are responsible in Romania and other parts of the world for children's villages, schools, education, medical care and healthcare, are being paid by congregations in Sweden. That includes, not least, the missionaries in Oradea, Lars Hörnberg and Lisa Egerbo. That provides maximum benefits for the children we have been given to care for," says Berndt Sanfridson.

The address in Sweden is:
Caminul Felix
Box 26
578 21 Aneby Sweden
The Visitor's Address is Industrigatan 41
Phone: +46 380 455 60
Plusgiro 90 06 49 – 5 (Romania)
Bankgiro 900-6495 (Romania)
Plusgiro 90 01 26 – 4 (Thailand)
Bankgiro 900-1264 (Thailand)
email: info@caminulfelix.se
www.caminulfelix.se

Chapter
29

'We Believe in Faith'

"The contact and collaboration between Caminul Felix's Swedish and International boards leads the development of Thailand's first family village," says Lars Hörnberg. "It is the incredible knowledge that the parents at Caminul Felix's villages in Romania and the board's members have which has now been transformed into building a Thai family village.

All the leaders and all the culture in Thailand is Thai, of course. The children belong to Thailand and the villages are tools for those who dedicate their lives to the children there. There is much experience in the group of leaders and parents. All who are involved in the villages are Thai.

The expertize that the international Christian Felix family village activities has includes concepts that are International, such as Mom and Dad, siblings and a home, care, respect, and love, as well as the resources for education, healthcare and a good standard of living. It is through this environment and approach that the role model of a family, for one's entire life, is being impressed into the children's lives.

We believe in faith. That is, faith in the children's rights, our responsibility and vocation and the special mission of our time to reach the children and provide them with a family and faith in God and life. Give the children faith and good values, and they will become believers and be safe and they will develop their creativity and talents. Faith in a good God always gives the best results.

The city of Surat Thani in southern Thailand was recommended by Görel Krohn as the site for this project. Görel Krohn was a missionary and the Swedish Pentecostal Movement's contact in the country. "Surat Thani is a big town with big needs," Görel said.

According to the testimonies of many, there are well-educated young couples there in the congregations who understand the need to care for abandoned children. One lands in Surat Thani, which is the main city, and then travels south to Hua Hin, and to Koh Samui and Koh Panagh, etc. In Surat Thani, there are good schools and hospitals. It is a developed city with good job opportunities. That is what a Felix family village needs for its children and families.

In Surat Thani, the village will have ten homes, with about 12 children in each. The family village is situated close to town, but is also separate from the bustling city life. Both in Romania and Thailand, Felix is building with the intention that they need to have access to life in town and, at the same time, to be able to be a bit separate both as a family and as a village. Being integrated into society and not cast out, but supported by the fellowship of family and the Felix village is very important.

This is a good idea. It is the only concept of life a child should be taught to live with. It is a child's right and our possibility to give. It is comprehensive in its contribution and it is a lifestyle. It is more than only food, or only a room. We find out what it costs, and then we try to pay these bills with support from all the good donors.

Now, it is happening in Thailand. Pastor Mana Rujirayanyong in Surat Thani is Caminul Felix's contact. Together with him as an interpreter and well-established community leader, Caminul Felix has seen a fine group of house parents coming together. Several young couples have shown the dedication of their hearts. "In Romania as well as in Thailand, it turns out that many people feel called to give their lives to become a Mom and Dad in Felix villages," Lars Hörnberg concludes.

Chapter

30

The Project Leader

Lisa Egerbo is responsible for the project in Surat Thani. As you know, Lisa is Lars Hörnberg's closest co-worker, and she has been a key person ever since the vision of Caminul Felix was announced in Falköping more than 24 years ago. "After all, I'd been the Hörnbergs' agent in Sweden!" Lisa used to say, "and it was absolutely certain that I was going to join in on the exciting journey that the vision had set out on."

Lisa's total commitment to the family villages in Romania has been, and is, impressive. Nobody knows how many journeys she has made in Scandinavia, England and the U.S. as a leader and interpreter for groups of young people who have grown up in the family villages.

I have been listening to their singing and testimonies and seen how the audiences have given large offerings to the unique concept that seems to spread to more parts of the world.

Yes, that is true, not only Romania and Thailand, but we are also talking about Uganda and Zimbabwe. Moldova has been on the horizon for a long time. Lisa and Lars are praying for more workers for the great mission.

Having now read this book, perhaps you feel that you would fit into this unique jigsaw puzzle of co-workers and tasks. Several people are already on their way to Thailand. A few of them will teach English while others help out with practical duties. Fences are to be built and lighting is to be installed on the compound.

As I am now writing this, Lisa has returned from yet another journey to her other great field of activity, Thailand. During the same time frame, she has also found time to visit both Norway and Sweden together with some girls from Sunflower Design in Oradea. "It's fun!" she exclaims enthusiastically. But our dear Lisa needs to take care of herself as well.

Berndt Sanfridson, Lisa Egerbo and Lars Hörnberg

As mentioned, Lisa is the project manager for the Felix Family Village in Surat Thani. Her closest co-worker in the village is Pastor Mana, whom you have met before in this book.

Many decisions need to be made and many details need to be discussed. You need to have two different foundations; one that owns the village and another that is responsible for the software, that is, the spiritual and humanitarian content for children and parents.

Legislation in Thailand does not allow a family to adopt more than three children. The houses have been built for twelve children. There, the children are not adopted in the legal sense, but for the children, the new family is like a real family.

"Very good schools and healthcare are available in town. That is how it is in Romania and that is how it is in Surat Thani. The children are being transported to school by the village's own vehicles.

Concluding Words

Many things have happened during the ten years since I tried in my book to describe the evolution of Caminul Felix in Romania and later on in Thailand.

In this English edition you have read about how the Caminul Felix adventure began, about the family villages that evolved, and how young couples decided to give their best years to abandoned street kids who would otherwise never have been able to manage a forthcoming adult life.

I have named these first parent couples and also briefly described their venture into the concept that has built Caminul Felix. It is definitely a unique concept in the world. Some of these parents have now given 20 years of their lives, raising hundreds of children into good citizens in society, making academic degrees or training for practical professions possible. Many of these children have now started families of their own and have had children of their own.

The first parents who came have become grandparents, and the family is usually able to count some 50 members!

The first 25 years of Caminul Felix stand as living proof that the world is not hopelessly lost.

Since then, new parent couples have come on board, and new generations of children and adolescents have grown up in a wise and warm-hearted atmosphere. A new generation has also begun in Surat Thani, Thailand, as well, and soon the first family village will be completed, with ten domestic houses for approximately 100 AIDS related children.

The importance of the Caminul Felix concept can never be

overestimated, and the young men and women who join this program become pillars of the society that is taking form after disasters such as the Ceausescu regime in Romania or the tsunami in Thailand.

Writing books has not been my main task in life! However, encouraged by Berndt Sanfridson and Lars Hörnberg, I nevertheless dared to take on this project. They have had confidence in me!

In order to make the book intelligible and easy to read, I would like to thank Elise Sanfridson. Elise has reviewed the text carefully, corrected my Swedish, and saved me from dangling modifiers.

Thanks to Jonathan Newton for translating the book into English, and Charlene Pagett and Wally Schoon for the great job with getting the text flowing.

* * *

Dear reader.

Thank you for coming along on this journey through different countries and people. You have met ordinary, decent people, who in their youth heard the voice of God and who decided to obey Him and lay their lives and their gifts into His hand. One was the son of a pastor, who came from completely ordinary home conditions where Mom and Dad had to watch every penny in order to make ends meet. Multitudes of friends donated financial gifts which were being administrated by a few, and the results are simply amazing.

I am not thinking primarily of the buildings in Oradea or in Surat Thani. I am thinking of the generation that was given the chance to grow up in the family villages and who have found their role in life today. They have started families of their own, and have in turn have themselves become donors and sponsors.

Dear reader, once again thank you for your gift to Caminul Felix!

But most important, give yourself as a gift to God, for He can use you!

Since this book was written many things has happened in the lives of Lisa Egerbo and Lars Hörnberg. Lars has described it in the following writing:

"I married Lisa at the end of December 2013.
What an incredible start of newness and beauty to my life. For that I thank God.

Lisa Egerbo moved to Romania at the beginning of the birth of Caminul Felix. She came with her rich personality and incredible talent. She is a blessing to the Felix Families in Romania and Thailand, and to the Eastern European Bible College.

We have become one in marriage and I enjoy a beautiful, sound and funny life companion. I love that fantastic lady Lisa Egerbo-Hörnberg."